INVEST YOUR WAY TO RICHES:
THE CONTRARIAN WAY

KETUL KOTHARI

ISBN-13: 978-1507818831
ISBN-10: 1507818831
ASIN: B00EBZHEWW

Printed in the United States of America

This book is dedicated to all investors, large and small, who are willing to learn the basics of the value / contrarian investment strategy.

Table of Contents:

PREFACE:

Notes by the Author

This book is a must-read for the amateur investor looking to learn how to consistently achieve above average returns by going against the crowd. The only way to achieve extraordinary returns is by acting differently than everyone else. This is what the contrarian way is all about.

The strategies introduced in this book are very similar to those practiced by many of the top investors of our time. Now with this easy-to-read book, you too can learn how to be a contrarian. If you are looking for a book filled with statistics and case studies, then this book is not for you. The purpose of this book is to help explain the world of investing and investments in a simple way that just about anyone can understand. It is also designed to help the reader to understand the mentality of a successful investor (this is the reason for the inclusion of some psychological biases and concepts).

The book should prove to be very informative and thought provoking for both current and aspiring investors alike. Even skilled professional investors will find this book to be an incredible resource for reviewing some of the basic strategies that can lead to above-average performance.

Before we get into actual chapters of the book, I'd like to share with you a story which describes to you my previous background and thought process when I was writing this book in the first place.

Growing up, my life was nothing special. I was born and raised in an average middle-class environment. I went to a public primary education system and attended a public university. All my early life, I was no one too special.

The only unusual things I had going for me was that I had a twin brother (no we're not identical), and huge future aspirations. I've always been the type of person willing to go the extra mile to learn more and get things done quickly.

What inspired me to write this book was simple. From an early age, I was excited by the concept of money and investments. I simply loved the concept that it was possible to have money that you already had be put to use to make you even more money. Majoring in Finance in college served only to bolster this excitement even further.

Investing is my passion. I've been following the capital markets since I was a teenager, and have no plans to stop doing so any time in the near future.

With my many years of experience, I'm in a unique situation to teach you, the reader, some of the tricks that I've learned both from reading books on the strategies of others, as well as my own strategies that I've developed over time. In total, I have thoroughly researched over 200 years of investment history and strategies when compiling this book. You'll find that some of the strategies are straight forward, while others are counterintuitive.

Becoming a successful investor really revolves on just three concepts. Picking the right investments, structuring your portfolio correctly, and having a strong enough emotional patience to disregard market fluctuations. This book will help you, the reader, to learn more about all three.

This book is broken down into three main sections. The first section focuses on introducing the reader to a general overview of the financial markets and market psychology.

From there, the second section focuses on actually introducing some core investment philosophies and concepts. This section, in particular, is what will arm the reader with the resources needed to spot potential winning investments.

Finally, the last section of the book is focused on portfolio structure. Picking all the best investments in the world mean nothing if you don't have a large enough position in any of them to actually get a good return. This section highlights the different strategies that you should consider using when deciding just how much money to allocate to an individual position.

That's it, that's all I have to say. The main event's about to start so be sure to grab some popcorn, snacks, and some soda. Notebooks and pencils are also strongly encouraged. It's time to get started....

INTRODUCTION:

Learning From Your Mistakes

"The definition of insanity is to do the same thing repeatedly and expect different results."

– Albert Einstein

Bulls versus bears, appreciation versus depreciation, profit versus loss. The world of investments is all about the two sides of a single equation. In the short term, under normal circumstances, when one person makes money, the other side loses money. There is no getting around this unfortunate reality.

The world around us is filled with investment and business opportunities. No matter who you are, or where you live, you are exposed to these opportunities every single day of your life. From the local business down the street to shares in the largest corporations of the world, there are potential investment opportunities nearly everywhere.

The key to successful investing is to learn to spot the best of these types of opportunities. Most people have their own flawed ways of looking for great investment prospects, whether it be chasing after the recent high-flyers or betting on falling trends.

Though sometimes profitable, these types of opportunities usually spell financial disaster.

The crazy part is that disaster after disaster people still continue chasing after perceived trends, unable to resist the temptation of making a quick dollar. This is a big mistake, yet one that is being made repeatedly, like clockwork.

The media has a lot to do with this clear irrationality. By highlighting high-flyers and repeatedly conveying a pessimistic outlook for companies with recent set-backs, this outlet serves only to hamper the ability to think logically.

At the end of the day, the media makes much of its money from the emotional response of people, so it is only fitting that it would focus on stories that evoke strong emotions. This is the source of the problem.

From my own personal observations and personal narratives from some of my close friends, I've noticed that many individual investors make these same types of amateur mistakes. My goal is to change this. This book was written to teach these kinds of people the tricks and psychology required to succeed as an investor over the long term.

The process will not be easy, but by reading this book, you'll be sure to learn a lot about investor psychology, corporate valuation, and accounting/financial metrics. You will also develop a basic understanding of special corporate events such as mergers and spinoffs.

So how can you measure the effectiveness of the strategies described in this book? That's easy enough. If you closely follow the guidelines described in this book and are able to outperform your peer group and the broad market index (S&P 500, Russell 1000, etc.) over the long term, then this book will have served its purpose.

Good thing for you, the reader, is that the strategies mentioned in this book have been thoroughly researched and proven to maximize the probability for outperformance. This, does not, however, mean that results are guaranteed.

If you aren't able to outperform (results depend on reader's ability to properly analyze companies), then all of your efforts will have been for nothing, as you could've matched the return of the broad market (before taxes and fees) by simply allocating your money to index funds.

Despite the risks of potential failure, reading the chapters ahead will best help you to obtain the knowledge necessary for a successful investment career.

PART ONE:

UNDERSTAND THE FINANCIAL MARKETS

Chapter 1:

Being a Contrarian

"Whenever you find yourself on the side of the
majority, it's time to pause and reflect."

– Mark Twain

With the recent memory of the housing
crisis still deeply etched into the minds of many, it is
very difficult to start any conversation on the stock
market today without referencing the steep fall from
the peaks of 2007 to the panics of 2009. That period
was one of the most fear-driven and unusual events
that I've ever experienced in my lifetime.

Now more than three years from the bottom of the
crisis, investors that bought into the S&P 500 near
the bottom of the sharp fall and held onto their
investments until today can look back at the scary
memory with a smile. They have more than doubled
their money.

Throughout my history as an investor, if there is one
thing I have learned, it is to avoid listening to market
pundits or so-called experts. If you're sitting there
reading this book with CNBC playing in the
background, you must turn it off now.

You won't need it anymore. In fact, it may be a
good idea to toss the television set out the window

or unsubscribe to the station entirely. Use that time to go out and personally learn more about the companies that you have invested in. If you've invested in a retail store, go and visit one of the retailer's physical locations and check for yourself the customer traffic at the store and the cost or quality of the merchandise.

There's no need for you continue watching CNBC only to get involved with dramatic headlines that distract you from the reality and obscure the facts. In fact, much of what is seen on financial news channels can just be considered "noise".

Investing should not have to be hard. You should not have to constantly be watching the news or constantly buying and selling securities in order to generate an above-average return. This may be what conventional wisdom teaches people, but conventional wisdom yields conventional results.

If you want to be the person that yields an above-average return, don't expect to achieve that by following the crowd. To become extraordinary it is absolutely necessary to learn to think differently, and one way to start is to avoid blindly following what is preached on financial news channels like CNBC.

If you are one of those people that has regularly watched CNBC or some other financial news station over the years, I don't mean to offend you. In fact, I too was once one of those people. I too was once one of those people that followed the recommendations of Jim Cramer on *Mad Money* or invested in hot stocks and hot industries. I too was one of those investors that found himself regularly losing money for reasons he couldn't truly understand.

It was through these repeated setbacks and losses that I came to the realization that I was following the wrong path and that a change of strategy was necessary for a successful investing career. The tricky part was that finding a better strategy meant that I had to first figure out the problem with my current strategy, and that would prove to take time.

My first encounter with a strategy in the right direction came when I took notice to an unusual peculiarity with the markets. I had become tired with losing money in the stock market and had decided it was time to take a different approach. In my quest to create a new investment strategy, I came across a very interesting realization.

Why was it that the biggest losing stocks of one year oftentimes proved to be the biggest winning stocks the following year? Why also was it that the biggest winning stocks of one year often failed to continue to do as well the following year or collapsed entirely? The only reasonable expectation was that the market often valued some securities based on unreasonable expectations and overreactions.

This, then, meant that investors could, theoretically, be able to capitalize on market overreactions exacerbated by the media, by viewing these opportunities as a chance to distance oneself from the crowd and conduct an independent analysis of the situation. If a fundamental and valuation based analysis of a company displayed positive results than this would present a good purchasing opportunity.

To further explain this logic, I'd like to explain to you what it took me many years to learn for myself: blindly following the crowd during periods of excess optimism leads to the downfall of most investors. There are very few exceptions to this general rule, and most exceptions are based on sheer luck or good fortune.

Why is it that the majority of amateurs and even so called sophisticated investors tend to flock to the same investments or group of investments right at the worst possible times? Some examples could be the investors that bought into Microsoft and America Online at the height of the technology bubble, when the world seemed like the stock market was made to make people very wealthy, and that these were "can't lose" investments.

In the words of Warren Buffet, one of the greatest investors of our time, this is what he would call following the "herd mentality". Always following the crowd is one of the greatest mistakes that an investor can make, and also the most common.

What results from excessive crowd following or the activity of everyone rushing in the same direction is the creation of extended market cycles. These growth cycles are fine and profitable for as long as they exist intact. However, when these bubbles eventually become overextended and burst, the crowd-follower is in for a huge surprise. He or she may find herself losing fifty-percent or more of his or her investment in a very short period of time.

> *"Always following the crowd is one of the greatest mistakes that an investor can make, and also the most common."*

Let's look at the example of Microsoft. At the height of the technology bubble the software company hit a share price as high as $58.00 a share, only to drop to as low as $22.00 a share as the bubble burst. That's a loss of over sixty-three percent!

Imagine the impact this type of loss would have had on someone that viewed the bubble as a way to make quick money and took the risk of liquidating his or her retirement account and investing in Microsoft at its peak. This type of investor would have seen his or her entire life savings fall by over sixty percent in the time span of a single year!

To make matters worse, these bubbles are often very difficult to predict beforehand, and usually are only recognized in hindsight. The bursting of the technology bubble at the early turn of the new millennium and the more recent housing bubble are just two examples of two types of bubbles that led to catastrophic losses for many investors.

The solution to avoiding this problem of blindly contributing to a bubble may be simpler than one might think. The most reasonable solution would be to become an independent thinker that does not follow the crowd and instead comes up with his or her personal viewpoint.

In other words, the solution is to become a contrarian, the same lesson that I learned after many years of experimenting with different investment strategies. It's kind of ironic how some of the most successful investors become so by breaking conventional wisdoms and widely followed investment principles.

So what is a contrarian? It's possible that many people new to the world of investing may have never heard the word before or understood its significance. A contrarian is someone who opposes or rejects the popular consensus based on an independent personal viewpoint or analysis. Some of the most famous investors in the world are contrarians.

Some notable examples include Warren Buffet, Peter Lynch, David Einhorn, David Dreman, John Templeton, and Mark Ripple. Seeing as these investors are contrarians, it should come as no surprise that successful investors like Buffet and Lynch often advocate for buying when others are selling and selling when others are buying. This philosophy is at the very core of the contrarian's strategy.

I'm sure you're wondering what exactly makes contrarian investors successful in the investing game. Well, contrarians are successful because they look at things objectively and pay close attention to specific companies or sectors that the market have overlooked, bought excessively, or sold off in a panic. Looking at these overlooked opportunities, for instance, means that contrarians might prove able to pick up shares of some companies at bargain prices well below reasonable long-term valuations.

Some of these bargains are often found in the aftermath of recent bubbles, when most investors are still fearful of entering back into the markets and have thus pulled out their money from the market and bid down the prices of profitable and quality companies. The emotional panic which ensues after the burst of a bubble can be the ideal environment for contrarian investors to find high quality investment opportunities at bargain valuations.

Contrarians are highly disciplined in their investment approach, and have specific investment principles which they use to analyze each case objectively. This is a very important aspect to have for success as an investor. Without a disciplined approach, investors may find themselves pulled in by the urges of the market---fear and greed, and it is these same emotions which have hurt the returns of many otherwise skilled investors in the long-term.

Hunches are an absolute no-no. It's okay to have a hunch, but a hunch should not be the sole basis for an investment. Before investing any amount of money to anything, it is absolutely necessary to have a valid well-thought out reason for making an investment.

At the same time, it is not necessary to always be completely invested in the market. If you are unable to find good investment prospects, than that means you should keep that money in cash until a good investment prospect appears. It's surprising how many amateur and even professional investors feel the urge to have to be completely invested all the time. There's no need for you to give in to these urges.

Being fully invested just for the sake of being fully invested is counterproductive as it may force you to allocate capital into a sub-par investment just to remain completely invested. At the same time, not having at least some amount of cash on the sidelines means you will not have the capital necessary to exploit unforeseen opportunities which may arise.

Contrarians also believe in the concept of focus investing, as a way to decrease the breadth of diversification and potentially increase overall returns. This concept of focus investing stands in

sharp contrast to conventional wisd
never put all your eggs in one o
Contrarians do just that.

They put most of their eggs in a s
group of baskets and then proceed to ₁ ₋ᵧ attention to
that basket very carefully. Also, because each pick
will have a huge impact on performance, contrarians
using the focus investing style will make sure that
they know their investment prospect very well
before putting in any amount of money. If you'd like
to read more about the focus investing style check
out *The Warren Buffet Portfolio* by Robert
Hagstrom.

Each and every security which is in a focused
contrarian's portfolio has been bought after thorough
research and sound reasoning. The portfolio is
comprised only with the investors best picks, all of
which have had capital allocated based on the
probability of investment success. This is very
beneficial because it means that you aren't diverting
capital into the securities of other companies just for
the sake of increased diversification, which is what
many inexperienced investors advocate for.

The probability of investment success is part-science
and part-art, derived from both fair-value
calculations and subjective assumptions on earnings
and revenue growth. The trick to picking successful
investments is to be as conservative with these
assumptions as possible. If after using very
conservative assumptions, an investment still seems

.gnificantly undervalued, than this presents a ...t investment to further look into.

It's important to keep in mind that no one in the history of investing has become rich by putting their eggs in many baskets. That's just not the right way for someone to become rich. In fact, that is probably the best way to remain poor by yielding only mediocre results.

Keep on buying companies that you know nothing about just so that your portfolio stays stable. But guess what? Your portfolio may be stable, but it won't be increasing in value anywhere near the rate it could be compared to more focused carefully structured portfolios. As an investor, you should not be unwilling to take any risks. Take risks, take even big risks if you have to, but at the same time, make sure that you learn to manage those same risks.

If you want to get above average returns, you will undoubtedly have to take some risks, but the trick is not in how big a risk you take, but on how you manage the risks that you take. When taking risks, it is absolutely necessary to manage risks in such a way that one or a few movements against you will not wipe out your returns excessively.

Hedging risks is an absolute necessity. That is the difference between being a successful contrarian investor that performs extraordinarily well over the long-run versus the risk-seeking investor that does very well for some time before ending up completely broke.

One more thing which contributes to the success of contrarians is that they always conduct their own research and are not dependent upon the analysis of analysts or other professionals. Doing their own research and doing it thoroughly are what allow contrarians to gather information on promising companies or industries that aren't either getting much media coverage or are getting negative coverage for reasons that don't impact long-term profitability---the hidden gems that are hiding in plain sight.

Because contrarians conduct much of their own research, it should come as no surprise that some of the greatest investors of our time conduct their investment research far away from the high-paced and informational overload regions of Wall Street. One of the best examples of this type of investor is Warren Buffet, who is hailed by many as one of the most successful investors of all time.

Warren Buffet lives in the calm and peaceful countryside of Omaha, Nebraska, far away from the financial centers of the United States. He is widely known to be high-tech averse and instead chooses to embrace simplicity and integrity. However, despite his humbleness and grandfatherly figure, his investment record is far from ordinary.

In the last five decades, Warren Buffet has outperformed the S&P 500[1] in all but four years throughout his entire investment career! In fact, $1,000 invested in the S&P 500 in 1956 until the end of 2007 would have yielded only $130,000, while the same $1,000 invested into Warren Buffet's Berkshire Hathaway would have yielded an astounding $30,600,000 by the end of 2007.[2] Talk about a substantial difference in returns!

The takeaway: contrarian investing allows for the potential for extraordinary returns, but the results will not be achieved overnight. The results also are not guaranteed because they depend on an individual's ability to look at and analyze companies and circumstances from multiple perspectives. This ability combined with a disciplined investing approach is what it takes to become a successful contrarian investor. Are you ready for the challenge? If you feel ready you can take the first step to a successful career in investing by continuing to read through the following chapters.

---

[1] S&P 500 refers to the index which is considered to be a benchmark for the overall U.S. stock market. The index is comprised of the top largest five hundred publicly traded companies.

[2] Statistics were derived from U.S. News & World Report, a recognized leader in fund and investment performance rankings.

Chapter 2:

Understand Market Irrationality

"The market can remain irrational longer than
you can remain solvent."

– John Maynard Keynes

The market is not always rational, nor is it always efficient. Those of you that are recent business school graduates may find this very hard to believe, but it is better if you learn this lesson sooner rather than later. If markets were truly efficient, than anomalies like the track records of Warren Buffet and some major hedge funds like Greenlight Capital or Renaissance Technologies should not exist. The very fact that these amazing long-term investment records exist undermines the validity of the EMH.[3]

Don't be so quick to believe everything that you learn in business school regarding the efficient market theory or even traditional investment principles. Not everything which is taught in school is correct all the time. Many professors and even professional financial advisors will have you believe

---

[3] EMH refers to the Efficient Market Hypothesis, a theory which states that stock prices reflect all information that is known by all investors, and thus that no single individual investor should be able to consistently outperform the broader market.

that stocks are the riskiest asset class amongst traditional investments, but even this widely believed principle is not necessarily true.

Why you ask? Simple, it is because risk is not constant. Just because bonds have historically held the perception of being "safe" investments does not mean that they will lead to stable returns going forward. Inflation is the biggest killer for bond returns, and there is always the possibility that an economy can experience a period of hyperinflation, thus drastically reducing the returns on fixed rate bonds. These same types of risk exist for stocks, for real estate, and even for commodities.

A good comparison for the idea that risk is not constant can be described through the notion that people had considered real estate to be a very safe investment even during the times building up to the eventual collapse of the mortgage bubble. At the time, most people were under the grand illusion that real estate prices always go up and never fall. Well, here's the reality: there is no asset or asset class where the value of the asset only rises and never falls.

This type of rationale is the result of a perception built up over time. If a certain asset class has done very well for a few decades, many people tend to forget that the value of that asset had ever fallen, and thus come to the false assumption that the value of that asset will never fall. As contrarians, we must learn to avoid these misconceptions. We must learn to always take a step back and attempt to look at an investment without any bias, understanding both the strengths and the weaknesses.

Markets become inefficient because they are impacted by the human emotions of fear and greed. When markets continue to rise rapidly for an extended period of time, people tend to feel more confident and greedy and start taking more risks than they normally would. On the other hand, when the broader market starts to rapidly decline they immediately panic and switch to become more conservative. These types of cycles seem to happen at least once every decade. Why is it that most people seem to continuously make the same types of mistakes repeatedly?

The best explanation is rooted in a field of study known as behavioral finance. According to behavioral finance theory, people tend to dislike losing money much more than the satisfaction they experience from winning money. It is an innate human tendency which affects everyone, although some people are more susceptible than others, especially if they are not aware of this tendency.

Emotions and psychology influence many aspects of our lives, and investing is no exception. Strong emotions can force people to behave in a manner that is irrational and oftentimes unpractical, and it occurs almost every single day in the real world. Consider how many people often go out to buy lottery tickets.

If we look at the practice of buying lottery tickets from a purely probability-based perspective, it makes absolutely no sense for anyone to buy lottery tickets as the chances of winning are roughly one in a hundred million. In fact, most people have a better chance of receiving a large sum of money through an inheritance from a rich uncle they barely know compared to the chances of winning money through a lottery ticket.

Despite this, millions of people across the U.S. regularly go out to buy lottery tickets, all inspired by the off-chance that they could win the lottery and become multi-millionaires overnight. It is this psychological urge and the thrill of the possibility of winning big that encourages people to act irrationally and it is an urge that is sure to remain in the future.

To better understand the activity of the financial markets, it is absolutely necessary to understand investor psychology and fallacies. It is for this reason that the next few pages will be dedicated to educating the reader about a few specific market anomalies that are routinely observed in the stock market as well as a few key concepts on behavioral finance.

To begin, let's start with the anomalies:

__January Effect__. This is a very well-known stock market anomaly. The anomaly has been thoroughly researched by statisticians and academic scholars and it has been proven that the month of January is a particularly good month for the stock market.

A part of the reason for this superior monthly performance can be attributed to the aftermath of tax loss harvesting. For those unfamiliar with the concept, tax loss harvesting is when investors look to reduce their total capital gains for tax purposes by offsetting the gains on their winning stocks with the losses on their worst performing stocks.

This tax loss harvesting practice leads to a selling pressure during the month of December that causes most stocks to fall in price despite their fundamentals and valuations as investors scramble to offset their capital gains before the year ends.

When the share price of companies with strong fundamentals falls far enough, these same stocks become attractive to investors in January, which can explain why stock market performance during the month tends to fare better than many other months on average.

Smaller Firms Outperform. When looking at the returns of individual stocks, it is easy to note that the stock performance of smaller firms[4] outperform the stock performance of their larger counterparts. This

---

[4] EMH refers to the Efficient Market Hypothesis, a theory which states that stock prices reflect all information that is known by all investors, and thus that no single individual investor should be able to consistently outperform the broader market.

effect should come as no surprise as smaller firms are bound to fluctuate more wildly in price because of lower trading volume and less analyst coverage.

At the same time, it is also important to keep in mind that smaller firms have the potential to grow much more quickly than companies that are much larger due to more room for growth in market share, expansion into other countries, and entry into new markets.

Although many of these same opportunities may be available for larger firms, revenue and earnings growth in smaller firms would have to grow much less than that of larger companies in absolute terms in order to end with the same change in growth as a percentage.

Post Earnings Announcement Drift. This anomaly references the phenomenon where the stocks of companies that post huge earnings surprise tend to drift in the direction of the surprise for a few weeks after an earnings announcement. This anomaly is in sharp contrast to the theory of EMT which emphasizes immediate market adjustment to new public information.

To date, the reasons for this anomaly are still not fully understood, but the most common explanation is that investors tend to initially under-react to large earnings surprise, explaining the performance drift that follows.

The September Effect. The month of September has widely been known as a historically miserable month for the broader stock market. The cause of this anomaly is not really understood, but part of the reason may have to do with the fact that some of the biggest financial disasters have occurred during the month of September. Some more recent examples include the collapse of Lehman Brothers in 2008 and the terrorist attacks of 911 in 2001.

However, despite these clearly dramatic events that have hurt the historical monthly performance, these instances alone cannot explain away the anomaly entirely. What surprises some people the most is that there is still a dramatic historical underwhelming performance even when the most dramatic events are factored out. This leaves many experts puzzled. It wouldn't be surprising if, for the near future, the true reason behind the September Effect remains a mystery.

Last Year's Losers Become This Year's Winners & Vice Versa. Statistical evidence supports the notion that the top performing stocks of one period tend to underperform the year after while the worst performing stocks of one period tend to outperform the following period. Although there is some evidence to support this anomaly, human psychology is sure to be one of the factors.

This is mainly because reversals may happen because people believe they will happen. If enough people start trying to sell one year's top performing stocks and start trying to buy the worst performing stocks, then this would encourage the respective stocks to move in the direction of the trading activity, turning the reversal into a self-perpetuating reality.

After considering all of these anomalies, it should be easy to understand that the stock market is not perfectly efficient, as there are quite a few inefficiencies which exist. However, the key to understanding the market is to understand investor behavior or psychology. To better understand the investor, I would like to now briefly talk about several tendencies and shortcomings of most amateur investors.

Anchoring. People are often influenced by information they've previously received. It is a very common fallacy; decisions are routinely made based upon irrelevant figures and statistics. Anchoring is a very powerful tool when it comes to influencing people's decision. Car salesmen successfully make use of this tool all the time in their efforts to encourage potential buyers to spend more on their vehicles. What's most amazing about this psychological trick is that it actually works!

When trying to sell something, initially mentioning a higher price than what you want actually tends to allow you to sell the same product for a higher price, on average, when compared to selling that same product without any sort of anchoring technique.

Talk about an effective and immensely useful psychological technique!

Before you go out trying to use the anchoring technique on everyone, it's important to keep in mind that people are susceptible to anchoring techniques at varying degrees. Some people, especially those with immense critical thinking abilities, are able to resist immediately accepting the information given to them. These types of people are less susceptible to the anchoring fallacy primarily because they are amongst the few that actually question the source.

As contrarians, it is very important for us to develop our critical thinking abilities as well as become more aware of the typical types of human fallacies. The trick is to be the person that not only understands human psychology, but also someone that is able to use psychological techniques on others rather than falling under their influence.

One very common example of anchoring is the notion that a diamond engagement ring should cost around two months' worth of salary. Strictly speaking, there is no reasonable basis for this "standard", yet the idea has become so engraved into the mind of the average person that people have started to actually use that standard when making decisions about which diamond ring to buy. Essentially, it is a nonsense benchmark that has been established by diamond jewelers over time in order to maximize profit and revenues.

So how does the concept of anchoring relate to the stock market? Well, because of the strong influence those current stock price quotations can have upon investors. When analyzing a company the current stock quote can greatly influence your estimations of a company's fair market value. For example, if the share of a company is trading at $100, and you estimate the company's intrinsic market value to be around $40, you are probably likely to question your calculations, even if you are right and the rest of the market is wrong.

You would probably find yourself wondering if you've calculated something wrong and constantly keep revising your calculations to come up with something much closer to the $100. Meanwhile, the true value of the company may very well be worth $40, but had gone well above this value due to strong speculation.

This is the impact that anchoring can have upon investors. On average, this "anchoring" of the current share price may lead you to come up with much higher estimates for the true value of the company even if you would have come up with an entirely different calculation had you not seen the current market quote. As contrarians, we want to avoid this shortcoming, so it is very important to make all attempts to ignore the current market quote when calculating the fair value for a company's shares.

Hindsight Bias. This psychological fallacy has to do with the idea that many people look back at the past and blame themselves for making obvious mistakes or failing to predict what could now be considered an inevitable event.

The reality is that many things seem to appear obvious after they have happened. This does not, however, mean that they were predictable at the time that they occurred. Many times people begin to unnecessarily blame themselves for past losses or huge gains that were missed because of observations they had chosen to overlook.

This is the type of situation that contrarians should try to avoid. Although some great opportunities may be missed, it is more important to keep looking, finding, and exploiting future opportunities instead of dwelling on the past. Basically, the past should not become a distraction for the present nor should it become a burden for the future.

Herd Behavior. Generally speaking, people love to be part of a crowd. They thrive on the sensations that involve feelings of belonging and commonality. For this reason, it should come as no surprise that many people have a tendency to mimic the actions of other group members. There are several reasons why this happens. One reason is because of the social pressure to conform. This social pressure can prove to be a very powerful force.

People want to feel like the group has accepted them, and therefore sometimes take drastic measures in order to fit in. The social pressure to conform is sometimes so strong that it could actually encourage people to lower their standards or principles and even compromise their ethical beliefs.

Another reason herd behavior is so common is because people tend to believe that while individuals may be subject to mistakes, the crowd is less likely to make mistakes. This is a complete misconception which many people are unaware of.

So why should you care about herd behavior when it comes to investing? Easy, because herd behavior is what allows you, the contrarian investor, to make money! If you wish to make money as a contrarian investor, then it is absolutely necessary to resist giving in to the urge to engage in herd behavior. Following the herd mentality is generally not a very profitable strategy because of the significant transactions costs that occur from constantly buying and selling securities to follow the latest trends.

When everyone is buying the same stock or the same group of stocks, herd behavior encourages others to also buy the same securities. This is the root of the problem. By following the behavior of the crowd, you will be forced into joining trends at a much later stage than the earliest adopters, especially because you will be joining into the investment "bandwagon" after the trend has already emerged. This is a serious mistake, as the strategy of the herd is not always correct, nor is it always profitable.

So now that you understand why engaging in herd behavior could potentially hurt your performance as an investor, let's learn how to exploit this human tendency for our own financial benefit. Herd behavior is harmful for the crowd follower but an amazing opportunity for the contrarian investor. The reason for this is because herd behavior often leads to the creation of attractive investment opportunities.

When the herd likes a security, that security will often be bid up to an unreasonably high valuation while when the opposite is true, the herd may bid down securities to ridiculously low valuations. To best increase the chances of making money, I advocate for betting on the ridiculously undervalued securities rather than betting against the overvalued ones.

> *"Herd behavior is harmful for the crowd follower but an amazing opportunity for the contrarian investor."*

This is because it is hard to predict when the irrationality of the herd will stop. In some special situations like in the build-up of asset bubbles, severely overvalued securities may continue to rise even more in price indefinitely.

This can place an emotional strain upon the mentally unprepared investor. As mentioned before, people hate losing money twice as much as they enjoy the sensation of winning money. Since the only way to bet against overvalued securities without using derivatives contracts like put options[5] is through short-selling[6], margin calls also pose a big problem.

For those readers unfamiliar with the concept, margin calls occur when investors have exceeded their borrowing limits on their brokerage accounts. The margin call is basically a demand placed by a broker asking the investor to deposit additional money or securities into the account so that the minimum account maintenance requirements are met.

The problem with betting against severely overvalued securities is that it could lead to losing more money than the amount invested, especially since the borrowed shares would be sold on leverage. If after selling borrowed shares, the value of the shares rose dramatically, then that could lead to debilitating losses!

---

[5] Put options refer to a type of derivatives contract which increases in value when the price of an underlying security declines in value. The opposite of a put option is a call option which increases in value when the price of the underlying security appreciates.

[6] Short-selling involves the process of selling borrowed shares from a brokerage in the hopes of buying back those same securities at a lower price and profiting on the difference.

Overconfidence. People have a natural tendency to think that they are more capable then they really are. If you don't believe it, you should go and enter a room full of people and ask them if they think they are an above-average driver. Chances are nearly everyone in the room will raise their hand. This brings up a very important question. If nearly everyone is an above-average driver, then where in the world are the bad drivers?

Although it can be useful when trying to impress or persuade someone, overconfidence is detrimental to one's actual performance. Feeling overconfident causes people to take more risks than they normally would since the decisions which the overconfident person makes are "always correct". This type of attitude is especially detrimental financially, when it comes to investing and stock picking abilities.

There's a very fine line between confidence and overconfidence. Although confidence in one's ability is very good and can lead to an increase in performance, overconfidence does not provide the same benefits. In fact, most investors and traders that are overconfident in their abilities eventually find themselves just a few trades away from a very painful wake-up call!

Contrarian investors would do well to learn from this psychological shortcoming. One way to prevent overconfidence from ruining investment performance is through discipline. Each contrarian should have his or her own set of specific investment criteria which must be followed at all times. It is through this intense focus and discipline that we can consistently avoid making preventable mistakes.

Overreaction. Emotions play a big role when it comes to the financial markets, and alongside emotions comes the tendency for people to overreact. The best part about these overreactions, especially in the stock market, is that they are often predictable.

This predictability can create various chances for profitable opportunities. Overreactions can cause the stocks of great companies to fall to unjustifiably low share valuations, while they can also push the stocks of below average companies to very high valuations. The reason for this clear mispricing of securities is due to fact that people tend to lean their decisions towards the latest information, making any change in opinion biased towards the latest company update.

To better understand this type of shareholder overreaction, let's consider a theoretical company called Company Z. Company Z has been established for over twenty years in a non-competitive industry and possesses a very strong brand image in its target market.

The company has consistently increased revenues and earnings at a decent rate of 15%-20% a year over the last decade. Recently, however, the company has experienced a set-back as Company Y, one of its primary suppliers, has experienced a fire that has damaged machinery in its primary manufacturing facility. As a result of this setback, Company Z has been forced to reduce its yearly product output, putting pressure on the company's annual sales and revenues.

Although the reduced output and decrease in sales for Company Z is temporary and forecasted to be resolved within the year, the share price of the company has declined by over 60% on the news, reaching an eight year low over the uncertainty. As can be seen in this hypothetical example, shareholders have bid down the price of this relatively stable company based on a temporary slump.

Yes, it's true that there is a fair amount of uncertainty involved, but the setback is unlikely to affect neither the financial performance nor the competencies of the firm over the long term. If contrarians ever came across this type of scenario in the real world, you can be sure that they would jump at the opportunity to buy shares at a bargain price, especially if the value proposition appears to be compelling. All that would be needed is for them to come to a final decision is some more thorough research on the prospect.

These types of overreaction scenarios seems to occur regularly in the real world, explaining why there always seem to be a sizable list of contrarian plays that could be made. This means that you, the reader, could also learn to exploit these types of opportunities, but you must first learn to think outside the box. Focus on the facts, not on hype or undue pessimism. Investors are myopic (near-sighted) and tend to focus on short term results. Rarely do they focus on long term trends.

To be successful, you must not think the same way as everyone else. It is important to consider the short-term, but the main focus should always be upon the long-term. It is the near-term view which tends to result in market overreactions and increased volatility over short periods, so why not reduce longer-term risk by exploiting the short-term volatility when it is so often predictable?

When it comes to investing in the stock market, strong biases are a god-send for the contrarian investor. Biases lead to irrationality and herd behavior, both of which can create some very profitable investment scenarios. If there is anything you should learn from this psychological shortcoming, it is to always keep a sense of reality or perspective when analyzing any new information you may encounter.

Try to avoid immediately accepting new information given to you as absolutely correct or error free. There may be some occurrence or aspect which other people may have overlooked, purposely left out, or outright ignored.

If you conduct your own research on an investment, and do a good job doing it, you may be able to uncover these overlooked aspects or information, creating an opportunity for high-probability and profitable contrarian plays.

The total return on these types of contrarian plays could very well surprise you! When it comes to conducting research two great sites to check out include *Seeking Alpha* (for financial news and analysis) and *Morningstar* (for financial metric information). Morningstar in particular is a very useful website site it allows for investors to easily comb through ten years of historical financial metric information.

Although understanding human psychology is very important when it comes to investing effectively, this does not mean that it is the only factor that you need to understand to become a successful investor. It is very important to learn from other people, especially other successful people. All great people have learned to adapt their strategies to fit their personalities, and you should do the same. Find your own way.

It can be a combination of a couple different strategies or it could even be the same strategy as someone else but with a slight twist. The type of strategy you choose to use is up to you, but one thing is for certain: you need to develop an edge, and so if you already have an edge, this is where it's going to be the most helpful.

PART TWO:

FORMULATE YOUR STRATEGY

Chapter 3:

Learning from the Greats

"The miracle is this – the more we share, the more
we have."

– Leonard Nimoy

The best place to learn to invest effectively
is from those that were successful before you.
Although this can be considered common
knowledge, it is surprising to see that very few
people heed this advice. Instead of trying to learn or
understand the investing strategies of famous
investors, they choose to pay excessive consulting
fees to financial planners and advisors. This practice
needs to stop!

Although there's nothing wrong with setting up a
consultation with a financial planner for estate
planning, insurance planning, or any other type of
financial planning, you should not set up
consultations for investment advice.

Most financial planners help you to achieve average
investment returns, but the thing is that anyone can
achieve average returns. Why should you pay huge
fees to a consultant when you can figure out how to
do average yourself? It just doesn't make sense!

Although these statements may seem controversial, they are based on significant truths. The reality is that not everyone deemed a professional is skilled enough to consistently achieve above average returns. If your goal is to become wealthy through investing, then a financial planner is not who you should go to for investment advice. Instead, you should choose to take the time to educate yourself.

Think about it this way, if you could achieve the same results offered by your investment advisor, and didn't have to pay the advisory fees, than you would be that much better off. Advisory fees can be substantial, especially since they are often structured as a small percentage of the assets under management. When dealing with smaller assets, this fee would not be as expensive, but when dealing with much larger sums, advisory fees can prove to be a huge drain upon your total financial returns.

Before realizing that many professionals don't have a market-beating strategy, I was in the same position as many of you. I too took the advice of "professionals" and gave my money to other people to manage. There is nothing wrong in doing so, but it is detrimental for your investment results. Once I realized this huge shortcoming, I quickly began to read books on investing strategies, especially any books written on successful investors with great long-term track records.

People like Warren Buffet, Joel Greenblatt, Carl Icahn, and Peter Lynch came to mind. This is where

I learned to develop my own investing technique by incorporating elements from the strategies of others, alongside some of my own ideas. Learning how to invest effectively is more about taking the time to educate yourself than it is about being lucky or taking on more risky positions, and the best part is that you can learn to do the same!

It's funny how so many people hand over their retirement funds over to someone else without even doing an ounce of investment research themselves. If you don't learn how to invest properly yourself, how can you know whether or not your investment advisor is acting in your best interest or is just trying to profit off of you? This is definitely something you should keep in mind. Most great investors follow a disciplined strategy, and for good reason.

Discipline helps you to make rational decisions based on sound reasoning instead of decisions clouded by emotion. Great investors don't just blindly make picks on what stock or group of stocks to buy without thoroughly researching them.

As a contrarian investor, you must do the same. Make informed decisions instead of following "gut instincts" or following what the crowd is doing. Do not be a trend follower, but a trend setter. Remember, it is easy to stand with the crowd, but hard to stand alone. Only when you are willing to stand alone will you live to see the wealth that so many people desire.

So, how can we as contrarians learn the investment strategies and practices of big-time investors? Well, there are quite a few ways. One of the ways is by practicing the same discipline as the billionaire investors. To do this, it is necessary to create a standard set of criteria or guidelines which each investment must satisfy in order to even be considered.

Developing this set of guidelines is not easy, and will probably take an ample amount of research to properly understand and put together. We need to figure out exactly what big investors look for when looking for investment prospects, and we can learn the basics for this by first learning more about fundamental and financial statement analysis.

For those unfamiliar with fundamental analysis, it is basically a method of using real data to estimate the true value of a security based on both qualitative and quantitative factors. It is the most widely accepted investment strategy and is generally used for longer-term investing, although it can also prove to be useful for spotting great short term plays.

When analyzing a stock, we essentially must follow the same basic criteria used when analyzing a business. This may seem like common sense, but it's surprising how often amateur investors aren't able to make this connection. Many people view stocks as abstractions. All they see are a bunch of symbols and corresponding numbers that rapidly move both higher and lower. They fail to understand that these random symbols and numbers represent the value of an actual business.

If we as investors want to understand whether or not the changing numbers correctly represent the value of the underlying business, then the first place we must look into is the financial and operating story of the business itself. To do this we can do quite a few things. We can read the company's annual report, visit some physical locations, talk to company insiders, and look at company financial metrics. Although there are many methods to analyze a company, for the purpose of this book, we will focus on the financial metrics.

So what kind of metrics do successful investors look at? Although there are many, some are much more popular than others. Here is a list of ten of the most useful financial metrics:

Return on Equity = Net Income/Shareholder's Equity

Return on Equity. This metric is all about how well the company's management is able to invest shareholder resources. The metric essentially measures the profitability of the business as it describes the return (as a percentage) that the company is receiving for each dollar of shareholder money that is invested. Good companies have very high return on equity such as above twenty-percent, while poorer performing companies may have much lower or even negative return on equity. Ideally, you want to own a company with a very high return on equity, the higher the better.

> Return on Assets = Net income/Total Assets

Return on Assets. This metric has to do with how profitable a company is in comparison to the total assets the company owns. Essentially, it is a calculation of the return the company is generating from the amount it has invested into capital or assets.

In an ideal scenario, you want to own a company that has both high return on equity and high return on assets. You also want a company that is able to generate a very high return on assets without a need for too much capital expenditure. These are the signs of a very healthy high margin business, one that probably holds a strong brand name and great barriers to entry.

> Return on Invested Capital = NOPAT / (Working Capital – Fixed Assets)

Return on Invested Capital. While return on equity measures how much of a return the company is able to generate upon one dollar of shareholder equity, this metric measures how well the company is able to utilize an influx of further capital. Joel Greenblatt, founder of Gotham Asset Management, is one prominent investor who focuses strongly upon this metric. In fact, he has actually created a systemic methodology on how to identify undervalued companies utilizing a company's return on investment and earnings yield metrics. This "Magic Formula" strategy has returned over 30% annual compounded returns over more than a decade. The strategy is described in great detail in Greenblatt's book: *The Little Book That Still Beats the Market*.

Debt-to-Equity Ratio = Total
Liabilities/Shareholder's Equity

Debt-to-Equity Ratio. This calculation is a measure of how much long term debt a company possesses in relation to the total amount of equity available. It basically indicates the proportion of equity and debt the company has used to finance its total assets and operations. Companies with high debt-to-equity ratios above eighty to ninety percent are generally considered undesirable, although there are some exceptions.

Also, it is important to consider that the debt-to-equity ratio may generally be higher in companies in certain industries as compared with companies in other industries. Ideally, you want to look for a company with a ratio below forty to fifty percent as this is considered a reasonable debt level.

Current Ratio = Current Assets/Current Liabilities

Current Ratio. This calculation has to do with how much cash a company possesses in relation to the total amount it needs to pay off short term debts and obligations. In essence, the current ratio measures a company's short term liquidity. The higher the current ratio, the better the company's ability to pay off its short-term debt.

When analyzing businesses, the minimum current ratio we should be looking for is a current ratio of 1.0 as this demonstrates that the company has just enough cash necessary to pay its immediate debts. Ideally, however, we would like to see cash-rich companies with current ratios of well above 1.0 such as 2.0 or 3.0.

High current ratios are especially common with some larger tech companies such as Microsoft, Facebook, and Cisco. This is because these companies don't need to invest too much capital and resources into assets or capital expenditure.

Free Cash Flow Yield = Free Cash Flow per Share/Current Market Price per Share

Free Cash Flow Yield. This metric is very important, because cash flow is the blood of any business. Cash flow has to do with how much money is coming into the company through earnings, commissions, and other sources relative to how much money is going out of the company through expenditures.

The free cash flow yield, in particular, is the percentage of cash flow per share that is expected to be generated in comparison to the stock's current market price per share. In an ideal scenario, you want to have a free cash flow yield of above ten percent, as this demonstrates that a business is able to retain much of the money it generates.

> Book Value Growth = Change in Book Value per Share over Five Years/Five Years

Book Value Growth. This calculation is one of the least used metrics, but also one of the most useful to spot companies with sustainable core advantages. The book value growth rate for a business measures how quickly the book value of the business has increased or decreased in value over a five year period. This metric is used extensively by Warren Buffet, one of the greatest investors of our time.

Book value growth basically tells us how quickly a company is able to build up its total tangible assets. The reason why it is so useful is that it helps us to identify companies that are able to increase their total assets without simultaneously increasing their liabilities (a potential sign of a company with a strong brand name or competitive moat).

Also, because book value growth may put a strain upon a company's financial resources, it is important to look specifically for companies that have managed to rapidly increase their book value without increasing their debt or diminishing cash positions.

If you can find a company with a high book value growth rate combined with cheap traditional valuation metrics, this is the ideal company to conduct more research upon. Such a company may be a good example of a profitable opportunity that the rest of the market may have not yet discovered.

Price-Earnings Growth Ratio = Price-to-Earnings Multiple / Expected EPS Growth Rate

Price-Earnings-Growth Ratio (PEG). This calculation is one of the best metrics to look at for making quick judgments about the valuation of a company. Typically, a PEG ratio of exactly one means that the company's shares are trading in line with its growth estimates. Anything higher than one generally means that the shares are trading at a premium valuation while anything lower means that shares are trading at a possible discount.

Although this is the general rule, there are quite a few exceptions. For example, companies with strong brand names or consistent earnings often tend to trade at slight to moderate premiums because of their perceived business stability and predictability. In some cases, two types of PEG ratios are used: one based on future growth assumptions (forward PEG) and one for historical growth rates (trailing PEG).

Payout Ratio = Dividends per Share / Earnings per Share

Payout Ratio. This fundamental metric is particularly useful for income investors. The ratio is generally used to determine the sustainability of a dividend paid out by a corporation. If a dividend payment exceeds the total amount of earnings generated by a company, then it is natural that the dividend of that company would not be sustainable as it would force the company to either drain its cash position or increase its liabilities.

Using the same line of thinking, if a dividend payment is well below the amount a company generates in earnings, than this type of dividend distribution would be considered to be much more sustainable. In an ideal scenario, income investors should look for companies with not only high dividend yields, but also very low payout ratios. Payout ratios of less than forty percent are considered to be particularly sustainable while payout ratios above eighty percent may not be as sustainable.

Short Interest Ratio = Short Interest / Average Daily Trading Volume

Short Interest Ratio. This ratio is mostly used when looking for short squeeze candidates. A short squeeze is a special situation where there is a rapid increase in the price of a security that is highly shorted due to a lack of supply and an excess demand for the security. This rapid increase in the share price usually occurs after a positive catalyst such as a large earnings surprise.

During a short squeeze, individuals holding short positions in a security are all forced to buy back shares to cover their existing short positions as the number of shares available for shorts rapidly decreases as more individuals rush to buy the security.

As more people cover their short positions, a trend emerges and the share price of the company's stock quickly moves higher. Although short squeezes may also be witnessed on the shares of larger corporations, it is most common on the shares of small-capitalization and mid-capitalization companies.

Profit Margin = Net Income / Total Revenue

Profit Margin. This calculation is very useful when you want to compare the quality of the profits generated by companies within a similar industry. Sometimes, earnings do not tell the whole story, especially when it comes to the long-term sustainability of a business. For example, a product company with higher profit margins than its competitors means that it is either able to sell products at a higher price than its competition or that it can control its costs of production better. Both of these are signs of a healthy business with strong operational efficiencies.

A company that is able to run efficiently may be able to effectively reduce the rate at which the cost of production increases, while other competitors may not be able to do the same. In an ideal scenario, investors should look to invest in companies that have high profit margins relative to their industry sectors. Profit margins in the high teens or above are generally considered to be especially strong, although these numbers may change drastically depending upon the industry the company is situated in.

Reading through the different metrics discussed above, many of you may be wondering why metrics like earnings per share or the famous price-to-earnings ratio were not listed. Well, there is a very good reason for this. One reason is because the important aspects of that metric are included in our PEG or price-earnings-growth ratio calculation.

Price-to-earnings (PE) and earnings per share (EPS) alone do not tell us much because without comparing the calculations to a company's expected long-term growth rate, we are unable to make adequate sense of the information.

Secondly, some of these metrics are also prone to manipulation. For example, earnings per share are particularly prone to manipulation by companies. Companies can increase or decrease the final earnings per share figure through accounting gimmicks, share repurchase programs, and other means. This manipulation is possible because the earnings-per-share metric is strongly influenced by the total number of common shares outstanding.

If a company wishes to improve its EPS for a quarter, it can simply speed up pre-approved share repurchase programs in order to decrease the denominator upon which net income will be divided. This maneuver can sometimes lead to surprisingly significant improvements in EPS even though the underlying business may not have improved at all over the same period.

The PEG ratio, on the other hand, helps to reduce the risk of manipulation because it calculates expected growth rates into the equation. Companies may be able to increase their EPS over time through share buybacks, but they usually are not able to adjust their expected growth rates.

By adding in the additional growth criteria, we are reducing the impact that manipulation has upon our calculations. It is for this reason that many contrarian investors tend not to focus too much on these two traditional financial metrics, and instead choose to focus on alternative metrics.

If you'd like to learn more about the different fundamental financial metrics that successful investor's look at, I highly suggest you check out *Creating a Portfolio Like Warren Buffet.*

Now that we understand what types of metrics successful investors look it, we need to understand where and how to come up with great investment prospects. With the tens of thousands of different possibilities out there, we need to figure out how to narrow down the possibilities to the most promising few. There are several ways to do this. One way is through the use of stock screeners.

Stock screeners are an incredibly powerful tool, and many are available for free. You can find stock screening tools on *Google Finance*, *Yahoo Finance*, online brokerage websites, and even through several business news platforms. Using these screening tools can help to quickly narrow down results to those with the most promising metrics. After filtering down the results to this narrowed list, it then becomes the responsibility of the investor to carefully analyze all of the companies on the list in order to identify the most promising investment ideas.

When analyzing these investment prospects, it is very important to look at not only the financial statements and metrics, but also the competency of current management, clarity of company annual reports, and the quality of earnings generated by the prospective company. Looking at previous operating history and historical average metrics can also prove to be very useful.

One resource that I find particular interesting is *YCharts.com*. This website provides many research tools that had previously been available only to the professionals. The only drawback is that the free version of the research tools have limited functionality so although it is still very useful, many important features have been reserved only for the subscription users.

Although this may seem like a tremendous amount of research, it really does not take up too much time. Additionally, taking the time to actually do this research will greatly help to improve your investment performance. If you want to become wealthy through investing, then it is absolutely necessary to do the type of research that other people are unwilling to do.

How else could you expect to uncover the great investment opportunities that the rest of the market has overlooked? A little bit of thorough research can go a long way when it comes to investing.

Besides the use of stock screeners, investment prospects can also be derived from carefully following the transactions of big name investors. Although not every investment made by a big fund manager or well-known investor may be a good one, the investments made by these types of individuals is definitely worth looking further in to.

High net-worth investors often have an entire team of research analysts constantly searching for good investment opportunities in the marketplace. Why then, should we not attempt to indirectly take advantage of this research by conducting our own research on the same companies or types of companies that these big investors have invested in?

There's really no reason why we should let this significant opportunity pass us by. By doing so, we would essentially be letting go of an opportunity to be able to quickly identify potentially undervalued opportunities and market sectors.

We might also be able to capitalize upon the influence of the big investors. A perfect example is the influence activist investors have over the companies they have invested in. Activist investors such as Bill Ackman and Carl Icahn are known for using their political and social influence in order to force management to act in a manner that unlocks shareholder value.

If we choose to invest in the same company that some of these activist investors have invested in, we may be able to piggy-back the benefit of their strong influence upon management and share price movement. This is one strategy that could make us money!

Big name investors are often known for their contrarian stock-picking styles, and we can use this similarity to our advantage. As contrarians, our goal is to make money investing, regardless of whether that means betting with or against the crowd, and to do this, one useful strategy is to track the transactions of either big investors or company insiders.

By doing this, we make our search for potential contrarian plays just a whole lot easier. If done correctly, you may find yourself on a path to great riches that you've never thought was possible. To learn more about how to track insider transaction please read onto the next chapter.

Chapter 4:

Tracking Insider Transactions

"Great minds discuss ideas; average minds discuss
events; small minds discuss people."

– E. Roosevelt

There are many different strategies out
there on how to achieve an above-average return, but
none tend to hold up as well as tracking insider
transactions. Tracking insider trades is nothing new,
and has been used as the basis for making
investment decisions for many decades. This makes
complete sense as there is no better place to generate
investment ideas than from the transactions of
company insiders.

The reason for this is because company insiders
generally have access to much more information
than we do. Their decisions to buy or sell their
company's securities may also be influenced by
their access to non-public information (although this
is supposed to be illegal).

Tracking the transactions of these insiders can prove
to be incredibly useful for the investor willing to
take the time needed to properly track these
transactions.

The Security & Exchange Commission[7] considers insiders to be company directors, officials or any individual with a stake of 10% or more in the company. Nowadays, tracking insider transactions has become increasingly easy. Websites like *Insider Monkey*, *Yahoo Finance,* and the 13F Filings on the Security & Exchange Commission's *Edgar System* demonstrate just how easy it is to gain access to this information.

Using these resources, we can track the insider purchases and sales of fund managers, high-net worth investors, company directors, and even company executives. All it takes to track this information is an internet connection and a few clicks with the mouse. The harder part, however, is learning how to make sense of this information.

The significance of every transaction is not the same, so some purchases and sales often prove to be much more significant than others. When tracking insider transactions, we should not make a judgment about a security just because a single insider has sold a small position. Insiders can sell their holdings for various reasons such as to fund new purchases, to diversify their holdings, or even to simply raise cash.

---

[7] The Security & Exchange Commission (SEC) is responsible for regulating and enforcing federal laws regarding the capital markets and electronic exchange markets within the United States of America.

What's more important than an insider sale is the quantity of that sale relative to the holdings of the insider. For example, an insider selling ten percent of his total holdings is not as significant as an insider selling seventy percent of his or her holdings.

Using that same logic, we can also consider why company insiders would purchase shares. While people might sell shares for various reasons, they usually only buy for one: when they expect to make money! Of course, there is always the possibility that an insider may be buying shares to improve confidence in the company's shares during a time of uncertainty, but in such situations insiders are very unlikely to purchase shares in huge quantities. To raise confidence in a security, insiders are much more likely to buy in small quantities as they themselves are likely to not want to lose money.

When considering insider transactions, we also want to look for the volume of insider activity. Not every insider may be skilled at identifying the true value of their company's shares nor may every company insider have the same information regarding the direction in which a company is headed. To make up for this unpredictability, the best investments to bet on or against would be those that have substantial insider activity.

If ten insiders have sold large amounts of their company's common stock over a short period of time, then this is a perfect example of a company we as contrarians may think about betting against.

Similarly, transactions made by chief executives should be given much more weight than transactions made by company directors.

This makes logical sense because those responsible for the strategic vision about a company tend to know much more about where a company is headed compared to someone only in charge of company operations.

The opposite case may also be true. If a large volume of insiders are shown to be buying the common stock of a company that has plummeted in recent months, then this could be the perfect contrarian buy signal. Many insiders tend to make transactions against the prevailing market sentiment based on longer term company expectations. We would be wise to make note of these transactions.

Besides tracking insider purchases and sales, we should also pay attention to transaction types. Sometimes, insiders may set up automatic programs to routinely purchase or sell company shares at specific regular intervals. These programs merit additional review.

We need to pay close attention to whether insiders have sold shares as part of their routine programs or have independently decided to sell a portion of their holdings. Although a minor issue, this is definitely something which should be considered when tracking transactions.

When it comes to tracking the moves of fund managers, there tends to be a slight drawback: hedge funds are only required to report their holdings within a forty-five day period following the end of a fiscal quarter. This is a significant amount of time.

A lot of things could happen between the time a position is initiated by a fund and the time the position is to be reported. However, this drawback does not mean that the delay would prevent people from being able to successfully generate an alpha[8] generating strategy.

In fact, a study conducted by the researchers at *Insider Monkey*, using data from 1999-2008, has shown that despite the reporting delay, mimicking the positions of hedge funds has historically led to beating the market return by an average of fifteen percentage points per year.[9]

This is a very big difference! An additional fifteen percent return over a nine year period means that investors would've made more than three-and-a-half times more money by mimicking hedge funds than they would have by buying a broad market index fund. Who wouldn't be happy with making triple the money that they did make!

---

[8] Alpha refers to a portfolio metric which attempts to calculate the return of an investment in excess of the security's expected return based upon the risk exposure.

[9] Source: "Hedge Fund Education Center." Insider Monkey. Web. 08 Feb. 2013.

Hedge funds, unlike individual investors, have access to a ton of resources they can use to find profitable investment opportunities. Because of their sheer size, hedge funds also take a much longer time to build up a position in a company. The case is not the same for individual investors. One of the biggest advantages individuals have over hedge funds is that they can invest most of their portfolio into smaller capitalization companies.

Hedge funds do not have this luxury as they have just too much money in manage. If these funds did attempt to invest a majority of their portfolios into smaller capitalization stocks, they would end up holding majority ownership of these companies.

With billions of dollars to manage, it makes more economical sense for them to focus more on "huge whales" to invest in. Mega-cap companies like Exxon-Mobil or large cap companies like Oracle and Cisco are some examples of the types of companies large funds would choose to invest in.

These types of mega cap and large cap companies tend to be much more stable in terms of share price fluctuations. They generally do not tend to move as much as small-cap and mid-cap companies in terms of their yearly fluctuation ranges.

Much of this fluctuation can be explained away by the facts that smaller companies tend to have much less analyst coverage and relevant public information, making them much less efficiently prices compared to their larger counterparts.

This poses a great opportunity for an alpha generating investment strategy. If we can already substantially increase our annual returns by following the transactions of hedge funds even after a reporting delay, imagine if we decided to combine that with only paying attention to a hedge fund's small-cap or mid-cap picks. The results of this type of strategy could have the potential to yield annual returns in the mid to high double digits!

Despite its tremendous potential, strong insider activity should not be the sole basis for an investment. You must still do a proper analysis on the company to come up with your own conclusions. The insider activity should only be used as a general guide to either screen for good potential opportunities or gain a general sense of what company insiders think about their company's future. Only then will you be able to objectively analyze company specific situations and come up with a logical reason for investing.

> *"Strong insider activity should not be the sole basis for an investment."*

Besides tracking insider transactions, it is also very important to consider how much of a company's shares are held by both insiders and institutions. A high inside ownership generally represents strong confidence in the company's prospects.

It also gives company insiders and executives a strong incentive to maximize value for shareholders so that the insider can profit as well. While high insider ownership generally tends to be good for shareholders because it allows for the goals of both groups to align, there is such a thing as too much insider ownership.

An excessive amount of insider ownership is harmful as it gives the company insiders too much corporate control. This, in turn, can cause the interests of management to differ from those of shareholders. This type of situation is especially common amongst corporations that have multiple classes of stocks. Because some classes of stock may have greater voting rights than the other classes, these "super shares" would make it less likely for insiders to be replaced even if they yield below average results.

The perfect example of this type of situation can be conveyed from the situation at Facebook in early 2013. Although Facebook has become a public company as of the year 2012, the founder and CEO, Mark Zuckerburg, has repeatedly shown that he cares more about the long-term strategy and success of the company instead of short-term earnings and revenue results. He owns roughly twenty-eight percent of the company yet has managed to retain a fifty-seven percent majority of the voting rights.

Because of this clear majority, Zuckerburg is not required to receive permission from shareholders or even the Board of Directors for any course of action he wishes to take. Also, considering his goals as the founder of the company, Mark Zuckerburg is likely to sacrifice short-term results in exchange for longer term sustainability.

This is the complete opposite of the interests of most shareholders. Shareholders generally want to receive benefits today, instead of the promise of a possible greater payout in the future, and this stands in direct contrast to the visions of many corporate executives. Another great example of this is the CEO of Amazon, Jeff Bezos, who has repeated shown to place a much higher value on long-term revenue growth, market share, and customer service then on quarterly or even yearly earnings.

Just as a corporation's insider ownership is an important aspect to consider, so too is the institutional ownership of a corporation. Institutions tend to have a strong influence upon the decisions made within many large companies.

However, the more large institutions hold the common stock of a specific company, the less likely it is that the shares of that company are inefficiently priced. Some of the best investments come from companies that are neglected, have low analyst coverage, or have very little to no institutional ownership. This is because the common stock of these types of companies may tend to be undervalued relative to their fundamentals.

Besides reducing the chances of a company being undervalued, institutional ownership could lead to strong buying and selling pressure based on important company specific events. This is especially true because most institutional investors tend to operate with short-term horizons rather than longer-term horizons.

Because institutional investors tend to purchase and sell their positions in large blocks, this could lead to sharp movements in the share price of a company's common stock, especially if many institutions start to sell or build up their positions at the same time. This is definitely a potential risk which should be considered when considering an investment in a smaller company with very high institutional ownership.

The above examples may have shown high institutional ownership to be an undesirable trait, but institutional ownership can also prove to be a very good thing. For instance, companies with relatively high institutional ownership tend to be much more liquid than those without it.

This becomes especially true for companies that are just becoming large enough to be included into new stock market indexes. Since index funds cannot buy securities that are not a part of their respective benchmark indexes, the addition of a company stock into an index can lead to a strong buying pressure as many index funds start adding shares of the company to track their respective indexes.

The index funds that buy the shares also serve as an anchor on the price since these funds will not sell their holdings in the firm unless the company proceeds to drop out of the index. In a sense, inclusion into stock market benchmarks helps to stabilize the downside fluctuation on share prices, thus helping to reduce annual share price variation.

This can be a strong benefit for investors without a strong stomach for price fluctuation, but at the same time, it also means a reduced potential for outsized returns.

Since our goal as contrarian investors is to maximize our returns, it would thus make sense to invest in non-index companies initially while managing a small capital base, and gradually switch to undervalued index companies as our capital base steadily increases. This strategy can help us to maximize our returns over the long haul.

It would also help to buy only when we consider a company to be significantly undervalued instead of just slightly undervalued. This can help us to increase the chances of getting outsized returns while reducing our annual portfolio turnover, commission, and tax expenses. We will be able to learn more about how to estimate the intrinsic or fair value for a company in the next chapter. However, before we get a feel for how to calculate fair value, it helps to have an understanding of the different types of investment strategies that are out there.

So what types of strategies are out there? Well, in all honesty there are quite a few. Some of the most common and popular types are listed below.

Growth Investing. This type of investing strategy surrounds investing money into securities that have been on a strong historic growth trajectory. Investors of this strategy tend to focus on companies with increasing earnings over a multi-year period, perceived strength of underlying corporate business models, and high potential for future share price appreciation.

When it comes to growth investing, most companies and investments that fall in this category are generally situated in "hot" industries like technology and healthcare (specifically biotech). For this reason, the return of this type of investment strategy can often prove to be unpredictable—varying widely between a return on capital of many times an initial investment or a complete loss of principal. What it ultimately comes down to is a disciplined approach and thorough analysis both of fundamentals and corporate management.

For those interested in learning more about growth investing, I would suggest reading more about the strategy of Phillip Fisher—often described as the "father of growth investing". One great read would be *Common Stocks and Uncommon Profits* written by none other than Phillip Fisher himself.

Value Investing. The goal of value investing is to identify securities that are undervalued or mispriced by the marketplace due to inefficiencies caused by investor emotions. Based on significant academic research, this type of investing strategy has the greatest potential for above-average returns over the long-term.

While the fundamental logic behind the strategy tends to remain consistent, it is important to note that there are many variations of the value investing strategy. There's deep value investing, contrarian value investing, and passive/active value investing. All of these types of value investing come with their own set of advantages and drawbacks. Deep value investing, in particular, is an interesting concept as this is the strategy first advocated by Ben Graham in the investing classic *Security Analysis*.

The goal of deep value investors is to purchase equity in public companies that are currently trading at a significant discount to their net assets and sometimes also their net cash values. This selection of deep value stocks is conducted without regard to the underlying profitability and operations of the company.

The logic here is that if the net assets on the balance sheet far outweigh the current market capitalization, then even in a liquidation scenario the investor should still come out with an acceptable return. While this logic may not end up becoming true for all deep value investments, on average, a basket of these types of securities should outperform the broad-market index over the long-term.

Compared to deep value investing, contrarian value investing appears to be the more popular approach amongst many of today's hedge funds and portfolio managers. Contrarian value investing is a strategy which revolves around using fundamental analysis techniques such as discounted cash flow analysis, normalized earnings projections, and cash flow / EBIT multiples to identify fair-value calculations for public companies.

Followers of this strategy would purchase the stock of companies that trade at a significant discount to their fair value calculations. It's possible for these discounts to have occurred for several reasons, including but not limited to short-term but fixable operational declines, market overreactions to pessimistic news, or the consequences of special situation scenarios. One of the primary characteristics of the contrarian value strategy is that the choice to purchase often contradicts the general market viewpoint.

DRIP / Income Investing. Compared to value and growth investing, this investment strategy is much better suited for those investors that are either highly conservative or focused entirely on generating portfolio income rather than on capital gains. In general, DRIP investors tend to focus on buying stakes in companies that pay regular and consistent dividends with above-average dividend yields. It's also a common practice for these types of investors to look into companies that have a track record for consistently increasing their dividends over time as this is a potential indication of a superb business with a possible sustainable competitive advantage.

Alongside researching into the quality of dividends, DRIP investors normally also set up dividend reinvestment plans to reinvest dividends obtained from their portfolios back into the respective dividend paying companies. The purpose of this process is to position the portfolio for greater future income generation.

For income oriented investors, building a properly structured portfolio is very important if one is to maintain a steady flow of income. A portfolio of dividend paying equities should include some solid core dividend paying companies along with other dividend payers from different sectors of the economy to enhance the stability of the income generation and reduce the impact of sector-related downturns. Some common sectors to look into include health care, transportation, utilities, consumer staples, financial firms, communications, and technology.

One valuable resource to check out for aspiring DRIP / Income investors is the *DRIP Investing Resource Center*. This website is fantastic for DRIP investors as it provides a compilation of all dividend paying companies that have paid consistent dividends for 25+ years in a row. The compiled spreadsheets are also broken out by region including a list of dividend champions from the US, Canada, and the UK.

GARP Investing. I've always found GARP investing to be fairly fascinating. This type of investment strategy is a type of hybrid between growth and value investing. GARP, or growth at a reasonable price, is a strategy which circles around looking for undervalued businesses that hold solid sustainable future growth potential.

Some factors with GARP investors look for include the growth characteristics of positive earnings growth over time, strong fundamental return metrics, and positive future growth estimates. At the same time, however, GARP investors also look for several value-oriented metrics including a strong focus upon fundamental metrics, reasonable valuation multiples, and realistic growth expectations. Most GARP investors, like value investors, shy away from aggressive growth companies such as those with growth projections in the high 20% or above. In the mind of GARP investors, these types of investments tend to carry premium valuations and are generally associated with greater risk and uncertainty. Instead, GARP investors generally opt for strong but modest growth typically within the range of 10-20%.

GARP investing is the primary strategy that had been utilized by the famous investor Peter Lynch during his 13 year investment career as the manager of the Magellan Fund at Fidelity. During this period, Lynch had averaged an enviable 29.2% annual return, cementing him as one of the great mutual fund managers of our time. Peter Lynch has also written a couple of books which are worth checking out including *Learn to Earn, One Up on Wall Street,* and *Beating the Street.*

Special Situation / Event-Driven Investing. Due to the complexity of analysis, this investment strategy is generally used only by the most elite and sophisticated of investors. Some examples of special situation circumstances include mergers and acquisitions, initial public offerings, reorganizations, spin-offs, recapitalizations, asset sales, tender offers, share issuances, reverse mergers, and bankruptcy proceedings.

During special situation circumstances, it is very possible for securities to become mispriced due to fundamental changes in valuation that occur at the time of the special situation transaction. At the same time, in many cases the special situation transaction can cause it to become very difficult to calculate realistic valuations for a company.

For example, if Company A has a partial stake in another Company B that is about to undergo an IPO, it can prove to be very difficult to determine what the true market price of the partial stake owned by

Company A should be. This complexity is part of the reason why special situations often allow for tremendous mispricing of securities, thus allowing for a great potential for large capital gains.

Now that we have an understanding of the different types of investment strategies out there, let's move on to the next chapter to learn more about the value-oriented concepts of margin of safety and valuation.

Chapter 5:

Margin of Safety & Valuation

"Price is what you pay. Value is what you get."
  – Warren Buffet

The entry point for an investment is one of the most important aspects of successful investing. The price at which you buy shares can make the difference between making a ton of money on a subpar company versus losing a substantial amount of money on a high quality company. As mentioned before, the stock market is not as efficient as many academicians may claim it to be.

Fear and greed lead to overreactions and often help lead to ridiculously low or absurdly high valuations. To best understand when and what is the right price to buy a specific company, it is important to understand and use the concepts of "intrinsic values" and "margins of safety".

Many of you that are new to the world of investing may have never heard the term "Intrinsic Value". Intrinsic value refers to the theoretical underlying value of a security that may or may not differ from the market or book value. The term is synonymous with "fundamental value".

> *"The price at which you buy shares can make the difference between making a ton of money on a subpar company versus losing a substantial amount of money on a high quality company."*

In reality, the intrinsic value of a company is by no means an exact number, as the valuation is determined not just by quantitative factors, but also by various qualitative factors such as management competency, trademarks, patents, barriers to entry, and copyrights.

In practice, the most common short-hand methods to estimate intrinsic values are by using discounted cash flow analysis or relying on multiples such as EV/EBIT, EV/FCF, or the price-earnings-growth ratio. At best, skilled investors and analysts can only come up with an approximate range for the intrinsic value.

Given this information, many of you are probably wondering how intrinsic value could be useful if it is not an exact number and at best only an approximation. Well, the reason why this type of approximation is useful is because intrinsic value is often viewed as a fixed approximation that does not change in value on a daily basis as does the market value for most securities. As the capital markets are emotion-driven, it is understandable how intrinsic value can come into play as a useful investing tool.

When times are well, and the economy or a company is booming, the market may value the securities of companies at a significant premium to their fundamental value. Similarly, when times are bad and the economy isn't faring as well, securities may often be selling at fire-sale prices, trading for well below their intrinsic values.

To see this relationship in another perspective, one may want take a look at Graham's Mr. Market analogy. The concept of Mr. Market goes something like this: imagine you are partners in a private business with a man named Mr. Market. Each day, he comes to your office or home and offers to buy your interest in the company or sell you his [the choice is yours].

The catch is, Mr. Market is an emotional wreck. At times, he suffers from excessive highs and at others, suicidal lows. When he is on one of his manic highs, his offering price for the business is high as well, because everything in his world at the time is cheery. His outlook for the company is wonderful, so he is only willing to sell you his stake in the company at a premium.

At other times, his mood goes south and all he sees is a dismal future for the company. In fact, he is so concerned; he is willing to sell you his part of the company for far less than it is worth. All the while, the underlying value of the company may not have changed – just Mr. Market's mood. [10]

---

[10] Source: Hagstrom, Robert G. *The Warren Buffett Way.*

Because the market is driven by emotions as is described by the Mr. Market analogy, skilled investors may find it in their best interests to utilize the concept of intrinsic value so that they can purchase securities at a discount, thus limiting the downside potential of their investment. The ideas surrounding the concept of margin of safety have been developed for this exact purpose: to reduce investment risk.

The concepts of margin and safety and intrinsic value complement each other. Individually, both concepts are incomplete and unable to help investors to consistently achieve above average returns. However, when properly used together, the results can be extraordinary.

So what is margin of safety and how is it used? Well, the margin of safety of an investment is basically the difference between the intrinsic value of a company's common shares and its current market price. In practice, the concept is used to buy securities only when they are trading at a specific minimum percentage below their present-day calculated intrinsic values.

This specific percentage may vary by industry or preferences, but ideally should always represent at least a twenty or more percent discount below intrinsic value.

Hoboken, NJ: John Wiley, 2005. 181-182. Print.

This "discount" is what protects the investor from any inaccurate calculations that may have been made with the fair value calculations. The margin of safety also helps prevent the investor from potential losses caused by market downturns. However, this does not mean that margin of safety guarantees a successful investment, because it doesn't. The concept is simply a tool which can be used, in combination with fair value calculations, to provide room for errors in an analyst judgment.

Although very useful when it comes to financial considerations, the idea of margin of safety is not reserved only for investments. In fact, the concept is prevalent throughout many different disciplines, structural engineering being one of them.

To better understand how the concept is used outside the world of high finance, let's look at the engineering considerations involved with building a bridge. Bridges are supposed to support more than 100 tons of weight on a daily basis. When engineers are designing a bridge's structure, however, they don't just shoot to support only 100 tons. Instead, they choose to design the bridge so that it can handle 140, 150, or even 160 tons.

> *"The idea of margin of safety is not reserved only for investments."*

This may seem surprising, but it makes perfect sense when considered practically. People want to feel comfortable when driving their cars over a bridge. A bridge collapse would completely obliterate this feeling of safety, as well as tarnish the reputation of the engineers that helped to build the bridge.

This type of situation, although unlikely under normal circumstances, can become possible should some unforeseen obstacle such as a natural disaster occur. Bridges have to endure almost every element imaginable.

Rain, snow, sleet, ice, heat, contraction, expansion, even the occasional hail. Engineers allow for a much greater weight capacity than is required simply to reduce the chances of structural shortcoming even if a special or unlikely circumstance were to occur.

Slight damage to the bridge's structure due to a hurricane or heavy snowstorm should not impact the bridge's minimally required capacity. This is the essence of the idea of a margin of safety. There should be no harm even if a highly unlikely event were to occur.

As someone that regularly reads through material from a multitude of different topics, I'm a strong believer in the idea that people can become better investors by incorporating some elements from other disciplines. Even some elements of everyday tasks such as buying groceries at the supermarket can prove to help people to become better investors.

The reason for this is because the same behaviors learned from shopping at the supermarket are applicable to the world of investing. When shopping for groceries, many people always look to buy products on sale rather than paying full price for them. Why can't investors look to do the same when investing? Why should people pay full price when they can get shares for a bargain? It makes no sense to do otherwise.

> *"People can become better investors by incorporating some elements from other disciplines."*

Although this idea makes perfect sense theoretically, the reason so few investors are able to apply this theory into practice is because of emotional considerations. Generally, the share prices of strong companies tend to fall below their respective fair values only when they are experiencing a rough patch or receive bad publicity. In these situations, most people are so scared of losing money initially that they let their emotions get the best of them and tell themselves that they will wait until the company shows signs of recovering.

This is the root of the problem. When a high quality company is experiencing a rough patch, the idea of waiting should not even come into your mind. You should quickly look to investigate the situation and invest in the company's shares if it appears to be significantly undervalued based on your intrinsic value calculations. These types of situations are especially common during periods of sector-wide declines, especially amongst companies in commodity-related industries such as mining, precious metals, oil/gas, and aviation.

Compared to other companies, businesses situated in cyclical industries tend to have wider and more predictable peaks and troughs during a normal business cycle. As disciplined investors, our goal is to identify the high quality businesses that may have fallen in the trough of a cyclical cycle. When these types of opportunities arise, we should not let the opportunity pass us by! This holds especially true for companies that are able to maintain profitability even during the worst portion of a downturn, as this would be an indication of an exceptionally well-managed business.

As contrarians, we should always be looking for high quality companies with great fundamentals that are trading well below their intrinsic values. These types of opportunities can prove to be immensely profitable, and it is important that decisions are made based on logical reasoning instead of based solely on emotion.

Valuation is the key to success. As contrarian investors, we always want to buy stocks that are valued at discounts and never stocks that are valued at significant premiums.

Slight premiums may be justifiable investments in exceptional cases, but never companies valued at significant premiums. Buying those types of companies is basically the same as simply handing over your money to someone else for free, something all contrarians should avoid if they want to succeed as an investor! You can learn more about the concepts of intrinsic value and margin of safety by checking out the bestsellers *Security Analysis* and *The Intelligent Investor* by Benjamin Graham.

Seeing as the concepts of margin of safety and intrinsic value are important, I would now like to demonstrate how these concepts can be used in practice. To do this, I'd like to walk you through a quick overview of the way a contrarian would analyze a company by giving a specific example: LinkedIn.

LinkedIn (NYSE:LNKD) is an online professional networking platform which allows members to create and manage their professional profiles. The platform also includes applications and tools to connect, find, and contact with business people, learn about career paths, research organizations, join industry groups, and pass on information.

Shares of LinkedIn are currently trading on the New York Stock Exchange at a price of $232.99 a share as of market close December 6, 2013. This share price translates into a trailing price-to-earnings multiple[11] of a little over 1,040 times.

---

[11] Trailing price-to-earnings multiple refers to the price multiple the

When this multiple is compared to the average price-to-earnings multiple of the S&P 500 which is currently above 15, it is easy to see that the market is currently valuing LinkedIn at a significant premium.

As contrarians, we now need to delve deeper to understand why LinkedIn is priced at a premium, to understand whether or not its business model will prove successful, and to understand management competency and ability to execute.

At first look, it seems apparent that LinkedIn is valued at a significant premium. However, investors are not ignorant enough to bid up the price of a company's shares without some type of reason. Looking into the company's earnings growth over the past few years, it is easy to see that the company is still in its aggressive growth phase.

In addition to that, it is also very important to note that analysts are currently expecting LinkedIn to grow at an average rate of nearly 60% over the next five years. From these findings, it may seem as if LinkedIn's exceedingly high valuation is justifiable. However, does this mean that LinkedIn is worth investing in?

What surprises me to no end is how many people buy into hype despite tremendously high valuations without even conducting even this basic preliminary

---

share of a company is trading at in relation to the sum of total earnings per share during the last year.

research. Some people buy shares of companies without a reason simply because "it's been going up".

Answering the question of whether or not LinkedIn is worth investing in is a very subjective question, and is thus open to individual interpretation, but it still requires some amount of preliminary research. To answer this question, we would need to take the time to understand just how many years of growth are already being priced into the share price, and this too would need to be estimated based on conservative forecasts and approximations.

Many people tend to disregard the importance of conservative forecasts. If analysts are estimating a growth rate of nearly 60% over a five year period, we should try to moderate that high growth rate by assuming a growth rate of 50% or 45%. The reason for this conservative estimate is to increase our margin of safety. When we factor in these conservative growth assumptions, the PEG ratio stands to increase even further than the 2.46 it is current valued at. This ratio shows that the company is undoubtedly valued at a significant premium.

The stock has incorporated at least ten years of growth into the share price. This is a significant red flag for an investment. Why should we try to buy LinkedIn at such a high valuation when we can just as easily find much better alternatives to invest in? Even some of LinkedIn's other fundamental metrics seem unimpressive. For example, both return on equity and return on asset metrics are insignificant at 2.05% and 1.80% respectively. Based on these three metrics alone, LinkedIn seems to be something which we should not invest in since there are likely to be better alternative investments out there. In essence, an investment in LinkedIn does not pass the opportunity cost test.

It is important to understand that there is still a possibility for someone to make money trading LinkedIn at current levels. There are some great positives for the company including expansion into other countries, new ways to monetize its business model, a growing user base, no company debt, strong cash reserves, and a very high current ratio at 4.71.

However, despite all of these clear fundamental positives, LinkedIn fails the most important one: the valuation test. This means that investing in LinkedIn involves a high degree of risk because the fundamentals of the company do not justify the price which the shares are trading at.

Although LinkedIn has managed to continually trade higher in recent months, these increases are based on a high volume of good news with respect to the company, and does not represent a change in the fundamental value of the company. With LinkedIn trading at such a high current-day valuation, any sign of earnings/revenue weakness or some other type of bad news may send the company's shares down dramatically, possibly down more than 50%!

As I've mentioned many times before, we should not let emotions get the best of us. LinkedIn is undoubtedly a great company, one whose services many of us may have personally used. The company is also currently rapidly increasing its earnings per share and expanding into new markets. This, however, does not change the fact that it is trading above its calculated intrinsic value, and therefore an unwise investment, especially from a valuation standpoint.

For this reason, I would recommend that investors stay away from this company, at least for the time being. If the company does manage to trade even higher than where its fundamentals currently justify, it would likely be based on speculation, something which all investors would be wise to avoid.

Chapter 6:

Investment Horizons

"An investment in knowledge always pays the best interest."

– Benjamin Franklin

When considering any investment, it is important to keep in mind how long you plan to hold your investment. Generally, the most profitable investments tend to come from holding periods of at least a few years, as shares are likely to appreciate much more in a time span of a few years compared to a time span of only a few days or months.

This is because it often takes time for the market to properly price companies that are significantly undervalued, especially if those companies are neglected by analysts and the market or have fallen out of favor. Longer term horizons also lead to greater tax benefits, making it easier to get the same net return as shorter term investments without the need for as much capital gains.

Under the 2013 U.S. tax policy, long term capital gains[12] are taxed at a rate of zero percent, fifteen

---

[12] Long term capital gains refer to the gains on any investment positions that are held for longer than one year.

percent, or twenty percent, depending on your marginal tax bracket. Short term capital gains, on the other hand, are taxed on a range between ten percent and 39.6% based on an investor's income tax bracket. This difference in taxation rates can make an incredible difference in net returns.

Using this comparison, it should now make sense why high-net worth individuals often lean towards longer term investing. By definition, any investment that is bought and held for less than a full year is considered to be a short-term investment while any investment that is bought and held for more than a full year is considered to be a long-term investment.

It is very important for people to understand the difference. I find it surprising how many people are unaware of this basic difference. Understanding the tax impact of different holding periods can help you to plan your strategy accordingly. In fact, I highly recommend that those individuals interested in investing in the capital markets take the time to learn more about the tax code. You will probably be surprised with all the different ways you can use to reduce your annual tax liabilities by receiving larger tax deductions and tax refunds.

Despite the benefits of longer term investing, this does not mean that you should never consider shorter term investment horizons. In fact, I would argue that the best strategy is to consider a combination of both. Short term investing can be a great way for investors to juice up their annual returns when they are lagging the market or performing below their respective targets.

It is also a great way to compound your returns and increase your wealth, especially when you are managing only a small capital base and looking to quickly grow your investment capital. The only problem is that investing both short term and long term will complicate your investment strategy as you will be forced to change your investment criteria based upon the investment horizon you decide to consider.

Those with longer term time horizons would be much more willing to wait longer for capital appreciation on their investments as opposed to those with shorter time horizons who want immediate results. Just as different investors have different levels of risk tolerance, different investors also possess varying levels of patience.

Everyone places different values on uncertain future returns. Despite these differences, I strongly believe that every investor's core portfolio should always be focused on the long-term. It's alright to dedicate a portion of your total portfolio to day trading or position trading, but this should not be the focus!

Day trading is basically a full-time occupation. If you're out there spending countless hours on the computer just to make some money, chances are you won't be able to enjoy any wealth you do manage to accumulate. Also, it's important to keep in mind that day trading stocks generally allows for very little capital appreciation on a single position.

This is because shares don't tend to appreciate as dramatically in a single day as they do over an extended period of time. Why go through the trouble of spending dozens of hours a week accumulating small daily gains when you could potentially get the same results spending putting in fewer hours? Personally, I don't find it a rational move, but I do understand why some people choose to engage in the activity. It can be a very lucrative career if done correctly.

Compared to day trading, I consider position trading to make much more sense from a time-based perspective. Being a position trader does not force you to spend dozens of hours a week carefully tracking minute-to-minute movements in the share price of a security. You don't have to be in constant emotional stress as every penny movement in either direction causes you to either lose or gain a good chunk of money.

In fact, with position trading, you could probably get away with checking on your positions once every few days. This can be very beneficial because you will have time on your hands to make money from other sources. You can have a day job, run your own business, or simply spend time developing a new skill. The choice is up to you.

The investment horizon you choose can make a huge difference on your overall investment strategy. Shorter term investment horizons may merit the use of technical analysis while longer term horizons merit the use of either only fundamental analysis, or both fundamental and technical analysis. For those readers that may not know, technical analysis is a security analysis technique which is often used by traders.

The goal of this analysis is to attempt to forecast the direction of security prices based on historical market data, specifically price and volume. Fundamental analysis, on the other hand, attempts to value companies based on its financial statements, competency of corporate management, competitive advantages, and growth expectations. If you wish to learn more about fundamental analysis, you should refer back to chapter three.

"The investment horizon you choose can make a huge difference on your overall investment strategy."

Since the basics of fundamental analysis are already described to a degree in several of the previous chapters, I would like to now take to time to go over some basic elements and guidelines for technical analysis. Again, it is important to remember that technical analysis is best for very short holding periods of a few weeks or less.

Here are some general guidelines for trading using technical analysis:

Stick to Your Trading Plan. Because strategies using technical analysis generally have very short investment horizons, it is absolutely necessary to have precise entry and exit criteria. If you don't strictly follow this plan, the chances of you losing money increase tremendously.

Day trading and swing trading require an immense amount of emotional patience and discipline primarily because there are sure to be movements of a few percentage points in both directions on a daily basis. If you close out a position too early, you could find yourself losing money on an investment that you could have made money on.

Conversely, you could also sometimes have made money on a position that is currently losing money. As long as you have a proper trading plan and good entry and exit criteria, you should be able to avoid having large losses on your positions.

Limit Orders vs. Market Orders. When getting into any position, it is important to use limit orders instead of market orders whenever possible. This becomes especially true if you decide to put in an order either before or after market hours.[13]

---

[13] Stock Market Hours are generally from 9:30 AM – 4:00 PM (EST). Although trades may be made both before and after market hours through after hours trading, for the most part trades will generally be executed on market open the following

The reason you should use limit orders is because with market orders, you don't know the exact price at which the order will be executed. For example, if you put in a market order to buy a security while the price is trading at $90.00, it's possible that the order could be executed at a higher price like $90.05.

Again, it's also possible that the order could be executed at a slightly lower price such as $89.95. The point is that market orders lead to some degree of uncertainty. This poses a problem for a trader managing a large capital base. The problem can be even more harmful when it comes to trading low volume securities.

Since the share price is determined by the volume of buy and sell orders in the market place, entering in a market order for a low volume security outside of market orders could cause you to artificially drive up the price of the stock based on your buying volume alone!

All of these problems could be avoided simply by using a limit order instead. While market orders are a command to a broker to execute a trade at the next available market price, limit orders instruct a broker to execute a trade only if a security is currently available for purchase or sale at a specific price or better.

Because there's a limit on the maximum price a trade could be executed at, limit orders are very

business day for ordinary investors.

useful to get into positions at a predetermined price (you know that when the trade is executed it will be for no more than the specified limit price). However, the drawback is that limit orders are not guaranteed to be executed unlike market orders which would be executed at the next available price.

Manage Your Losses. Just as limit orders are a very useful tool for traders, so too are stop loss orders. There are three different types of stop loss orders: stop loss market orders, stop loss limit orders, & trailing stop loss orders. All three types of order are designed to limit an investor's loss on a security position, but do possess some minor differences.

Stop loss market orders are orders placed with a broker to sell a security when it reaches at or below a certain price. Stop loss limit orders, on the other hand, are basically stop loss market order combined with the typical limit order.

Basically, a stop loss limit order tells the broker to sell a security at a specific price or better only if the security reaches at or below a certain specified price. The benefit of a stop loss limit order over a stop loss market order is that the former specifies the minimum price at which the security should be sold. This could prove to be very helpful for trade planning purposes.

Finally, traders can also use trailing stops to help manage losses on their trading positions. Trailing stop loss orders are similar to stop loss orders as they help limit losses on existing positions.

The difference, however, is that while normal stop loss orders have a static stop price that does not change, trailing limits are dynamic and automatically adjust the stop limit price closer to the market price when the market price moves in a favorable direction.

This type of order can be especially advantageous for positions that have been rapidly increasing in value. Because the limit price on a trailing stop will continually adjust to a specific percentage below the current market price, this means you get to keep more of your profits you've made.

When it comes to managing losses while trading, the general rule is to set a stop loss order for up to 5-10% below the current market price. The reasoning behind this is that there needs to be some amount of room for normal share fluctuations.

A 5-10% stop loss order allows enough room for daily fluctuation, but also ensures that you will not lose an excessive amount of money. If nothing else, I believe it is in the best interest of every investor to begin to start using limit orders and stop loss orders regularly if they do not do so already.

Analyze Trends. When it comes to short term investing, understanding market sentiment and trends is a big component. The first step is to identify exactly what type of market you are currently in. You could currently be in a bull market, a bear market, or even a flat market. The term "bull market" generally refers to a market that is either rising, or expected to rise in the near future.

A "bear market", on the other hand, is the exact opposite. Bear markets are associated with market conditions in which security prices are falling and surrounded with pessimism and negative sentiment. Finally, flat markets are associated with a market that isn't really expected to move much in either direction. Flat markets are generally a trader's worst enemy.

So what are some specific ways that technical analysts use to analyze market trends? Well, there are quite a few different ways. One way is to compare the moving averages on the major exchanges, notably the Dow Jones Industrial Average and the S&P 500. The most commonly used moving averages[14] include the 10-day, 20-day, 30-day, and 50-day moving averages.

When the 10-day moving average is higher than the 30-day moving average, then this is an indication that the market is generally moving higher. In the same way, when the 10-day moving average is lower than the 30-day moving average, then this is

---

[14] Moving averages refer to the average price of a security over a set period of time. They are generally used to identify market trends, possible areas of market support/resistance, and measure momentum.

an indication that the market is generally on its way lower, at least during the near term.

At the same time, another aspect to consider is where the share price of a company holds in relation to one of the shorter term moving average such as the 20-day or 30-day. If the current share price of a company appears to be either significantly above or below the 20-day moving average, then is could very well be an indication that the price could make a potential large move. The reason for this is simple: the price of a company simply cannot remain disconnected with its moving average for an extended period of time.

A great way to visualize this relationship is the example of a rubber band. While a standard rubber band could be stretched to be several hand lengths away from the original distance, at some point when the pressure is released, the rubber band quickly snaps back into place. The same could be said for the price of a security. While prices may on occasion depart widely from a short-term average, it will eventually fall back in-line with the average either as a result of the passage of time or a rapid price move.

From the above examples, it should be clear that moving averages are a useful tool for getting an idea of which direction the market is expected to move. However, even more useful than moving averages are the methods used to measure market volatility. Strong volatility and trading ranges are a trader's dream. When the market moves rapidly, huge profits can be made in a matter of days!

There are several ways to measure volatility and market sentiment. The most common ways include looking at the Volatility Index (VIX) and the Relative Strength Index (RSI). While the volatility index is often called the "fear index" because it tends to move in the opposite direction of the broader market, the Relative Strength Index is used mainly to measure the velocity of price movements based on volume.

The RSI is measured on a scale from 0 to 100. When it reaches 70 or above, the market is considered to be overbought, and you can generally expect prices to decline. When the index hits 30 or below, than this is considered to be a great buying opportunity as the market is considered to be oversold.

When it comes to analyzing candle-stick chart patterns, one useful resource is *Finviz*. This website is great for technical traders as it screeners for technical chart patterns, volume and fundamental stock metrics, and various other criteria.

Be Aware of Strong Catalysts. No matter what type of short-term investment you are looking at, you should always take into consideration any upcoming potential catalysts. Quarterly earnings announcements are one such catalyst.

Other catalysts could include changes in fiscal or monetary policy, unemployment rate announcements, tax policies, jobs numbers, or any other notable event that could affect market prices. It's very important to keep all known potential catalysts in mind when it comes to short-term investing.

The reason for this is simple, if there is some major announcement made during your holding period, you could experience some unexpected price appreciation or depreciation. This could prove to be a potential risk factor for your performance.

Of course, any unexpected price appreciation would be great, but there's also the chance that you could experience significant price depreciation as well. For this reason, it's best to try to minimize this uncertainty by at least taking the time to place important dates onto your calendar—especially for catalysts that are known and likely to materially impact your current open positions.

Trades Don't Always Work Out. No trader makes money all the time. You will always experience some trades that don't work out as planned for unpredictable reasons. The trick is to create a system and stick with it, as well as cut your losses whenever possible.

It's better to worry more about things you can control than to stress over the little things outside of your control. Regardless of your time frame, you should always have your entry and exit strategies known in advance. Whatever you do, you need to know in advance when you'll get out so that a small loss doesn't turn into a huge loss that you may never be able to recover from.

> *"You will always experience some trades that don't work out as planned for unpredictable reasons."*

Buy Low, Sell High. This advice is so common that nearly everyone with any idea about the capital markets has probably heard this one at least once. There's a strong element of truth to this advice. However, the problem is that many investors and traders find it very difficult to actually practice this rule in the real world. It's very difficult to try to time the bottom for a security that is quickly falling in value, especially when considering a short-term time horizon.

However, if done successfully, investors that manage to buy low and sell high stand to make a substantial amount of money in a very short period of time. Personally, I feel that this strategy would work best only when combined with the fundamental concepts of intrinsic value and margin of safety as discussed in chapter five.

Capital Allocation Limits. When trading securities, especially for the short term, I would advise not to allocate more than 10% of your portfolio for trading purposes. This ten percent of your total portfolio should then be broken down again into five, six, or more trading positions, and each trading position should never exceed more than 2-3% of your total portfolio.

Of course, you can always relax these rules when you're managing a very small capital base, but these criteria hold especially true when you are managing a significant amount of capital.

The reason for allocating only ten percent of your portfolio for trading purposes is because trading should only be a measure to juice up your annual returns, and not your core investment strategy. As a contrarian investor, there will always be some times when your performance will trail the broader market. Occasional short-term trading can help to improve your performance during these types of performance set-backs.

It can also sometimes be a good idea to engage in stock option[15] trading, especially with excess profits that you'd like to use to compound your returns. Although there is the possibility of losing all or most of the money invested into options, options can have great payouts if done effectively. Payouts of 200% or more are easily possible.

---

[15] A stock option is a contract which is sold from one party to another. The contract gives the purchaser of the stock option the right, but not the obligation to either buy or sell a stock at a previously agreed upon price within a certain period until expiration.

When it comes to equity options, there are two primary types: put options and call options. Put options rise in value when the price of the underlying security depreciates in value, while call options rise in value when the underlying security appreciates in value. There are also many different strategies, spreads, and maneuvers that can be used in conjunction with options.

Some of these types of strategies include covered calls, married puts, bull call spreads, bear put spreads, protective collars, long straddles, long strangles, and butterfly spreads. While this book will not discuss the various option strategies in detail, you can learn more about option strategies by checking out *The Options Playbook* by Brian Overby.

While utilizing options can be very profitable, I would advise most investors to stay away from writing options of any nature. Profitable or not, writing options expose you to a much different risk to reward ratio compared to simply purchasing option contracts.

They also lead to the use of more complicated strategies that may or not be suited for all investors. For this reason, I recommend leaving core option-writing strategies to the professionals, especially if you are unwilling to put in the time and effort to thoroughly understand option strategies as well as the respective risk management measures and practices.

While the maximum you can lose from purchasing options is the initial principle, writing options can expose you to virtually unlimited loss if executed incorrectly. This is a type of situation which all investors and traders alike should do their best to avoid if possible.

Now that you understand some basic guidelines and techniques for short-term investing, it's time to learn more about how exactly your portfolio as a whole should be structured. Investing in the right securities means nothing if these positions are not large enough to actually impact your total annual portfolio return.

Knowing how to properly structure your portfolio may be just what you need to gain that edge needed to outperform your fellow investors. To learn more about how you should structure your portfolio to best increase your chances of outperformance, read on to the next chapter.

PART THREE:

THE MAKING OF A CONTRARIAN

Chapter 7:

Structuring Your Portfolio

"Concentration is my motto – first honesty, then industry, then concentration."

– Andrew Carnegie

Being an extraordinary investor is all about concentration and focus. You should focus on buying only what you understand. If you don't fully understand an industry, then you should not invest in it! If you can't reasonably understand the risks associated with a particular investment, then why take that risk at all? Following this basic philosophy will save you from many unnecessary losses as an investor.

If you really want to get involved with a particular asset class or invest into a complex industry, then the first thing you should do is take the time to educate yourself. You should have at least a general understanding of what you're getting yourself into. Otherwise, it makes no sense to get involved at all.

There are many people out there that fall for the countless get-rich quick schemes out there. You will not be one of them. You don't have to invest your money into some obscure industry or some unheard of financial instrument just to get above average returns.

Let other people make that mistake. You should not. By taking the time to read this book, you've already taken a first step in the right direction. Now all you have to do is keep reading, and start applying what you learn. Do this, and better investment results should follow.

> *"You don't have to invest your money into some obscure industry or some unheard of financial instrument just to get above average returns."*

When it comes to investing in the stock market, the first step is to find great companies run by strong management. You then want to make sure that you are buying the shares of these great companies at a reasonable price. This is where the concepts of margin of safety and intrinsic value come into play (refer to chapter five). By buying companies at a sizable discount to their fair values, you will be able to reduce your downside exposure. Again, this is what makes all the difference in terms of performance.

Ideally, you never want to invest the majority of your money into more than ten to fifteen companies in total, especially when managing smaller portfolios. Having positions in any more companies then that will significantly reduce your chances of out-performance. Instead of making more money, diversifying your bets too much will only lead you to make less money while reducing your total portfolio variation.

There's nothing wrong with stability, but if you're looking to become rich through investing, you should always try to expose yourself to at least some degree of volatility. Only then can you truly get amazing returns on your investments.

Here are some great tips you should keep in mind when managing your portfolio:

Invest in Only Your Best Ideas. I cannot begin to describe to you how often I come across people that advocate for investing in companies or industries they know nothing about just for the sake of increased diversification. This type of thinking is a mistake! It makes absolutely no sense to add positions into companies you know little about, especially if you're willing to take the time to carefully research the companies that you invest into at a detailed level.

Think about it this way. If you were to carefully study only a select universe of companies, then you would be able to develop a much in-depth understanding of those businesses and the industries that they are situated in. With enough research, you may even be able to identify the primary strengths, weaknesses, trends, and opportunities of the industry, thereby positioning you well to discover future winners in the industry.

This in-depth knowledge could also potentially serve you when making future investments in other companies with similar products or business model—even those that are not directly related to the prior investments you may have made. In essence, by taking the time to thoroughly understand a business, you would not only increase your understanding of business in general, but also increase the likelihood of better future investment performance.

From there, you may even want to take it to the next level by limiting your investment prospects to the industries and companies that you know best and then focusing to gradually learn more about other industries to increase your knowledge base and areas of competency.

Concentrate Your Bets. Why put money into your twentieth or thirtieth best idea when you can just use that money to add to your position in your top five to ten ideas? Wouldn't that make more sense? It's surprising how so many people put money into ideas that they know probably won't perform that well, just for the sake of increased "diversification".

This type of thinking is counterproductive. If we try to divert our time and resources into analyzing and researching dozens of investment prospects, we are unlikely to ever develop an in-depth understanding of any of them.

This poses a huge problem because it is being better informed which gives contrarian investor's an edge over other investors. If we divert our time and energy into researching dozens of different companies, than it should come as no surprise that we will lose our informational edge over others, especially when it comes to analyzing hidden or overlooked aspects of a specific company.

It is for this reason that it is much more effective just to focus on the ideas on which you have the strongest conviction or those that show the highest probability of success rather than chasing after new positions just for portfolio stability.

Academic research has shown that holding a portfolio of just fifteen positions allows you to have approximately 85% of the diversification benefits of holding all the stocks of a broad market index. If we can achieve most of the benefits of diversification by holding fewer positions, it would make no sense for us to waste money on commissions by entering into any more positions than required.

Conventional wisdom tells us that it is unwise to put all your eggs in a single basket, but then again, conventional thinking yields conventional results. If you are looking to become rich through investing, then it should make perfect sense that you'll need to do things differently from everybody else. One way to do this is by concentrating your portfolio around carefully selected positions, and then proceeding to watch that portfolio closely.

> *"If you are looking to get rich through investing, then it should make perfect sense that you'll need to do things differently from everyone else."*

Don't listen to other "market pundits", "financial advisors", or "portfolio experts". Although some of these people are skilled at what they do and know what they're talking about, but the vast majority of them do not. Many will never be able to understand the benefits of a focused or concentrated portfolio, especially one that is managed properly.

In their minds, any type of portfolio concentration is never a good thing, even if it could mean much higher returns than any other strategy. These types of people are those that have been brainwashed by the traditional academic concepts of diversification and reduced volatility. Business schools across the country are to blame for this phenomenon.

These institutions often tend to force the ideas of the efficient market theory and modern portfolio theory down into the minds of young business students, leaving them unable and unwilling to consider alternative portfolio strategies. It's a shame, because many of the biggest and greatest investors in the world became successful investors by disregarding these very same academic theories. If you wish to become a successful investor, I would advise you to do the same.

Find your own way, one that works for you. The guidelines in this book can help you to develop your own way, but your own strategy can have all, some, or even none of these concepts. It's only when you find your own strategy that you will live to see results that you may have never imagined.

Think Long Term. Whenever you enter into any position, you should always take a look at the long-term sustainability of the underlying business. You should never buy a security based on a hunch, speculation, or on a whim. This holds especially true for any position that is to comprise a large portion of your portfolio.

Making an investment based on whim is the type of behavior that screams for financial disaster. Don't give in to the temptation for a quick profit, especially when you're thinking about making some money by trading the shares of a company with very poor fundamentals.

Although you may be able to make money on this type of trade, if the trade goes wrong even once, you could find yourself losing much more than all the profit you may have been able to accumulate over time.

That's like trying to pick up quarters at a casino. Sure, you can make some money doing things this way, but there are much better ways to make money. Debt-ridden and unprofitable businesses could very easily find themselves unable to meet their current liabilities. If this type of company ends up filing for bankruptcy or bankruptcy protection, you'll find yourself immediately losing ninety percent or more of your investment within minutes.

Quite frankly, this is not a gamble you should be willing to take, especially if you're looking to achieve extraordinary returns over the long haul. I understand that the temptation for a quick buck can be strong, but is the potential risk worth it? That is the question you should ask yourself before considering any type of short-term trade.

Trading is a great way to improve your annual returns, but if you do engage in short-term trading, you should only focus on trading the shares of companies with both good fundamentals and a reasonable valuation. This is the best way to help reduce your potential downside risks.

Increase the Size of Your Bets as the Probability of Success Increases. People seriously need to start thinking in probabilities. Thinking in probabilities will make it much less likely that you will give in to your emotions when making financial decisions. If you believe the market has overreacted based on some bad news and pushed down the price of a security well below your fair value calculations, it may be a good idea to increase the size of your bet on the position.

This becomes especially true if the underlying company demonstrates exceptionally strong fundamentals with little to no risk of bankruptcy at any point in the near future. It's like the concept of counting cards.

You always want to marginally increase the size of your bets as the chances of success increases. Many people think that falling share prices dictates an increase in the level of risk on the investment, but this is not always the case.

Sometimes share prices can detract from the fundamentals of the underlying business and fall due to speculation. These types of situations pose great investment opportunities. The problem with determining probability of success, however, is that it is very subjective. It is part art and part science.

However, despite the subjective nature of determining probability, it still helps to allocate your bets based on a specific weighting system. For example, if you believe a certain investment to have an 80% chance of success, you should definitely put a larger position into that investment compared to another investment that you consider to have only a 60% success rate.

This makes perfect sense from a logical perspective, and it could be a great way to help better manage the longer term risks of your portfolio. For determining the exact amount of capital to place into a specific position, I strongly recommend the use of the Kelly Optimization Model.

The Kelly Optimization model is pretty simple, and the success of the model is highly based on your informational advantages. The more you know about a particularly investment or company, the better this model will tend to work out for you. Its formula is listed as $Y = (2*P) - 1$, where the P represents the calculated subjective probability.

This means, that if you expect a particular investment prospect to have a 60% rate of success, you should invest up to $(2*.6)-1=.20$, or up to 20% of your total portfolio into that position. By doing so, you should be able to maximize your total return given the level of risk. Instead of the Kelly Optimization model, some people also advocate for the use of a fractional Kelly model, such as a Half Kelly.

The only difference between these two models is that you would invest only a fraction of what the Kelly Optimization model suggests that you should. This means that under the Half Kelly Model, you would only investment 10% of your total capital into an investment prospect which you believe to have a 60% rate of success, instead of the original 20% as calculated earlier.

The Half-Kelly Model is best suited for investors with weaker stomachs who are not able to stomach the amount of volatility associated with the Kelly

Optimization Model. However, because the Half-Kelly Model still allows for substantial investment returns, I think it may be the better choice for most investors.

Reduce Portfolio Turnover. Why pay more money to Uncle Sam than you have to? Taxes and commissions are a big area where many investors finding themselves giving away some of their returns to others. If you can do something to reduce the total amount paid in commissions and taxes, then your performance would be that much better off.

Ideally, it is always a good idea to have a big chunk of your portfolio in long-term investments. Sure, rapidly trading in and out of securities could potentially make someone a lot of money, but this large portfolio turnover, also increases the total amount paid in both commissions and taxes on capital gains.

Decreased portfolio turnover can also have some hidden benefits. For one, holding positions for a longer time allows for much greater capital appreciation, as well as possible increases in dividends. It can also allow more time for turnaround plays to work out, as well as more time to develop a deeper understanding of the industry and company that you've chosen to invest in. These things can become especially useful should you ever consider investing within the same industry again sometime in the future.

Recognize Psychological Biases. If you haven't already, I strongly recommend you look over the anomalies mentioned throughout the second chapter. These stock market anomalies are a great starting point for helping you to spot and exploit psychological biases both with investing and other aspects of life. If you can learn to recognize these psychological tricks, you'll be setting yourself up for great success at the investing game.

There is a very specific psychological mindset that successful investors tend to have. Successful investors will focus on probabilities and economic issues, and let decisions be dictated by logical thinking rather than emotional. If you too wish to become successful at the investing game, it's in your best interest to try to learn and apply this mindset.

Know When to Sell. If nothing else, it's very important to ignore market forecasts. There will always be people out there that are eternal optimists or eternal pessimists. There will always be those people that repeatedly claim that a recession is right around the corner, even when there are few signs of economic weakness. There will also be some people that will claim that the market will head even higher after it has already run up dramatically in a relatively short period of time.

All of these forecasts are simply "background noise", and none of these forecasts should influence your decision to either buy or sell. You should sell an investment you have a strong conviction for only if there is some instance or event that changes the fundamentals or the fair value of the business in a significant way. Valuation is the key to successful investing.

If the share price of your positions rise well above your fair value calculations (typically by thirty percent or more), then this is a much better time to sell. It's much better to sell based on a set of specific rules and criteria then it is to sell based on the market/economic outlook.

Buy What You Know. When picking any prospective investment, it's important that you are able to properly understand the business/industry that you are looking to invest in. Over the long run, companies in easy to understand businesses and industries tend to fare much better than their complex counterparts, especially from an investment standpoint.

Consider investments in obscure industries like biotechnology or certain technologies. Although there have definitely been some great potential investments in both of these industries, for the most part, companies in these sectors have fared poorly over the long term as a group.

Companies in the consumer durables and food/beverage industries, on the other hand, have shown to fare much better long-term. Under this logic, it should come as no surprise that companies like Coca Cola and Proctor & Gamble have fared so well throughout the decades. Both of these companies operate in relatively easy to understand businesses, surrounded by strong brand names, and both demonstrate a very steady increase in the flow of annual income over time.

The trick to investing successfully by buying what you know is to look for the opportunities that most others have overlooked. While everyone else is looking at the hot stock or industry that's currently under the spotlight, as contrarian investors, we should look for the well-known companies that seem to fallen out of favor or have been neglected in recent months. Here, is where we will be able to find the potential five baggers or even ten baggers.

Think Like You Own the Business. People that own their own businesses tend to think much differently from many investors and traders. While traders and short-term investors are only looking to make a quick profit, business owners are looking to create a sustainable income stream. As contrarian investors, it would be beneficial for us to think like business owners. If we do, we should find ourselves more willing to ride out short-term fluctuations and set-backs.

By thinking like business owners, we also would find ourselves willing to spend more time researching the industry that we've invested in and analyzing the strengths and weaknesses of direct competitors. All businesses have their own strategies, business models, and financial situations, and since buying shares in a company is basically the same as becoming a part owner of the business, it should make sense that we should try out best to understand the company that we've put our money into.

When it comes to any business, patience is a virtue. Investing is no different. While this chapter should have given you a rough idea of how to properly manage and structure your investment portfolio, the next chapter will outline the importance of patience when investing. To learn more, be sure to read on to the next chapter. You may be surprised by what you read.

Chapter 8:

Shareholder Value

"He that can have patience can have what we will."

– Benjamin Franklin

There are two kinds of people in the world. Those that expect everything to work out for them immediately, and those that are willing to wait and work hard to allow for things to fall in their favor. When it comes to the investing game, those that are willing to wait and conduct the necessary research to develop a detailed understanding of a business are the ones more likely to become successful investors. The reason for this is simple. Big fundamental changes and opportunities for a business rarely happen overnight. There is always a sequential and logical aspect to the development of any significant fundamental change.

Usually, big changes happen as a result of a large quantity of smaller incremental changes that have gradually accumulated over time. It takes a lot of time to actually create something of strong value or create something that will actually have a strong impact on people.

Creating value is all about strategic trade-offs. To accomplish one thing, you may very well have to sacrifice another. This is the purpose of developing a strategy in the first place. Wherever there is an opportunity, there is always an opportunity cost. This is the regrettable yet undeniable fact of the world we live in—yet one that is so regularly overlooked.

Many large mega-cap corporations are well-known for their attempts at creating value. For example, there is Apple, a company known for selling a variety of products ranging from phones to televisions. Apple uses closed ecosystems on its diverse portfolio of products as a way to better control and enhance the end-user experience.

By using closed ecosystems, Apple is basically sacrificing the user's ability to customize the products they've purchased. It also allows the company to simplify processes and maximize product security and reliability. This is a great trade-off that has allowed the company to create value by distinguishing itself from its competitors.

In addition to creating value for customers, trade-offs are also great for creating competitive moats around certain businesses. The reason for this is due to the perception of specialization, luxury, reliability, or a multitude of other branding factors.

There are so many other examples of famous niche-based companies known for creating customer value. Companies like Walmart, McDonalds, Monster Beverage, Fossil, Crocs, & Southwest

Airlines are some other great examples. All of these companies are well known within their respective industries, and some of these companies also boast industry leading profit margins and returns on equity.

> *"Wherever there is an opportunity, there is always an opportunity cost."*

Okay, so now it should be clear that there is a need for strategic tradeoffs when it comes to creating value for a company. But what about creating value for shareholders? How can that be accomplished? Well, here are some of the methods that are occasionally used by corporations in order to increase the long term value of a company for shareholders:

Buying Growth. If a financially strong company has reached a point where its natural growth is beginning to slow, it may be a good idea for such a company to consider buying growth through acquisitions. This strategy, although useful, does come with its own set of benefits and drawbacks. Let's start with the benefits.

Acquiring other companies, products, or product lines could create a great potential opportunity for increasing growth. It can also help to stabilize company revenue by diversifying revenue streams. These opportunities could serve as great catalysts for a company's share price.

As favorable news begins to be introduced to the marketplace, the share price of company shares should begin to appreciate accordingly, thus benefiting shareholders. Share prices tend to move based on news, so if there is greater volume of good news than bad news, then share prices will generally tend to appreciate. Conversely, if there is a greater volume of bad news, then share prices will depreciate in value.

Despite its many benefits, buying growth does involve a certain degree of disadvantages. One of the main drawbacks is the risk for improper integration and execution. Sometimes when companies start to acquire companies that depart from their core businesses, these newly acquired companies end up becoming a financial drain upon the parent company. This phenomenon has often been called *"diworsification"* by the famous investor Peter Lynch.

Although acquisitions can be great for the parent company if executed properly, this is not always the case. Sometimes situations may arise where the existing management of a newly acquired business is unable to continue to run the business efficiently.

Reasons for this could be multi-fold, ranging from a clash in corporate cultures to system integration issues. For this reason, it is important for company management at the acquiring company to understand the risks of an acquisition before even getting involved in any potential discussions. It would also be a good idea for both sides to attempt to retain the best management from both businesses post-acquisition.

Spin-Off Noncore Businesses. Spinning off the non-core businesses of a public corporation can be a great way for a company to create greater value for its shareholders. In a spin-off, a public corporation takes a subsidiary, division, or a part of its business and separates this portion from the parent company in order to create a new independent company or organization. These unrelated businesses could be spun off the parent companies so that the public market can better appreciate the newly formed companies.

Generally, a fast growing small division of a very large public company is largely ignored or valued at a discount by the market as a small division is unlikely to substantially impact the financial results of a large company. However, if this type of small division were to be spun off into an independent company, the fast growing division is very likely to get much better recognition by the market and thus be valued at a much higher multiple as a result.

A similar case can be made for the spinning off of underperforming businesses. Underperforming or problematic businesses detract time, money, and energy away from developing or growing the core business. Who wants to deal with an underperforming business segment filled with complex legal issues, large cost structures, or possible environmental issues?

In such cases, it would be wise to consider spinning off the underperforming company segment in order to create the best value for shareholders. As the underperforming segment is removed, the market will be much more likely to reassess the financial situation of the parent company and adjust the market value accordingly. This would lead to a greater total cumulative market value for the two newly separated entities.

However, spinning off business units from a parent company does come with its share of downsides. A few examples of downsides for this type of transaction include a reduction in overall corporate revenues and a possible decrease in sales mix diversification. The impact of these downsides should be carefully considered before an underperforming segment of a corporation is spun off from a parent company.

While in most situations the benefits of a spin-off should outweigh the drawbacks for strong businesses, there may very well be some cases where this is not the case. This is the reason why corporations employ teams of consultants and corporate strategists to crunch the numbers to determine cost-benefit analyses before conducting any type of major financial transaction.

Now that we have seen two different types of situations where spinoffs may be warranted, let's consider some of the possible tax benefits involved with a spin-off. One great tax benefit is that spin-off distributions can be made tax-free to the parent company and even to the shareholders that are part-owners of that same company. This creates a great tax benefit for the parent company compared to selling the subsidiary or division outright to another company. The reason for this is that an outright sale to another company would lead to the realization of taxable income for the parent company, and possible taxable gains for shareholders if this new capital is distributed via a special dividend.

The above scenario shows us exactly why spin-offs often prove to be very efficient from a tax standpoint. Instead of putting up an unprofitable division for sale, it would be best to simply spin-off the division into another company. Doing so could potentially unlock greater combined market capitalizations for both the parent company and the newly formed organization.

In addition, the parent company would then be able to focus on its core businesses while the newly formed company would be able to re-brand itself and gain the flexibility needed to turn itself around financially.

> *"Spin-offs are very efficient from a tax standpoint."*

This type of situation could be a potential win-win situation: a win for the two now separate companies as well as a win for shareholders. If you are interested in learning more about the different rules and regulations which must be followed for a tax-free spin-off, I would encourage you to check out the IRS website. You could also check out Green Blatt's book, *You Could Be a Stock Market Genius*, if you are interested in learning more about special-situation investing.

Issue Dividends. I am a strong advocate in the idea that corporations should avoid issuing dividends if it's possible. Although dividends are great for income-oriented investors, companies that issue dividends should only do so if they believe that it would be very difficult to make good use of that money elsewhere.

Companies that earn high returns on equity, have little or no debt, and possess tremendous room to expand in either their current industry or in international markets, would be best served to avoid paying dividends.

Instead, it would make much more sense for them to reinvest all of their excess capital into company resources in order to expand the business. Instead of simply distributing out cash to shareholders, that money could be used for introducing new products, experimenting with new technologies, increasing advertising expenses, increasing R&D budgets, or even acquiring complementary businesses.

The point here is that there are wide arrays of other opportunities that can be exploited. Cash should only be distributed out to shareholders if the benefits of any other available opportunities are not substantial enough to merit further investment. Handing out cash to shareholders in the form of dividends is one of the simplest things that can be done as it involves no creativity and no strategic tradeoffs.

In fact, it also leads to negative tax consequences. While reinvestment into company resources would lead to very little tax consequences, the issuance of dividends means that shareholders will be taxed on that income. This is something which should be considered before any dividend is considered by company management.

Initiate Share Repurchase Programs. While dividends should be avoided when possible because of its tax consequences, share buy-back programs could prove to be a much more beneficial alternative. As compared to dividend issuances which are taxable, share repurchase programs generally are not taxable. If a company uses the same amount of money to buy shares or pay dividends, then the total value of the firm will prove to be the same after either transaction excluding taxes.

When it comes to share repurchase programs versus dividend distributions, it is taxes which leads to a major inequality in favor of share repurchase programs.[16] Whereas dividends are taxed as ordinary income in the year they are received, any share price appreciation that results from a share repurchase program will be taxed as capital gains (usually taxed at a much lower rate than ordinary income depending on a share-holders income tax bracket).

Understanding this relationship, it should come as no surprise that a growing number of companies have recently been shifting away from dividends and instead choosing to engage in share repurchase programs. The net gain for shareholders proves to be much better under the latter, although receiving cash directly always seems to bring people more psychological satisfaction.

> *"When it comes to share repurchase programs versus dividends, it is taxes which creates a major inequality in favor of share repurchase programs."*

---

[16] Share repurchase programs are able to help appreciate share prices because they lower the total amount of shares outstanding for the company's common stock. By reducing the share count, but maintaining the market capitalization, each individual share price increases in value to equal to the same total market capitalization as before the shares had been repurchased by the company.

Reduce Operating Costs Where Possible. Any reduction in the amount of money spent on operating expenditures would have a direct impact on the bottom line. This is why it's so important for company executives to try to make the operations at their respective companies as efficient as possible. The more money that the company is able to retain, the more it is able to create value for shareholders.

The extra retained earnings could be used for various purposes including increases in dividends issued, larger share buy-back programs, more acquisitions, and possibly even a larger budget for research and development. All these purposes could help to increase the long term value of the company for shareholders.

So what are some ways to reduce operating costs? There are many different strategies that vary widely in effectiveness and relevance based on the varying business models of different types of companies and industries. Some examples of cost control measures include developing economies of scale, outsourcing payroll and non-key projects and processes, investing in technological advancements, pushing inventory management responsibilities to vendors (for product-based businesses), or possibly reducing the employee headcount.

Diversify Revenue Streams. A key principle on which the financial health of a company can be analyzed is the stability of its revenue streams. For a company to truly develop a strong long-term sustainable business, it is absolutely necessary to find as many ways as possible to diversify its sources of revenue and/or income. It is also highly important for corporations to find ways to generate strong flows of recurring revenue streams. One-time revenue generations do not contribute to the long-term sustainability of a business.

Revenue mix diversification and stability can often be achieved by entering into new markets (emerging markets for example), formalizing multi-year contracts with customers, engaging in licensing agreements, and/or entering into new product/service categories.

All of these measures can have a significant impact on a company's revenue stability and diversification. For example, while a company that only sells its product in its domestic market is likely to be strongly impacted by a severe downturn in that country's economy, a multinational company with product sales in over fifteen countries is much less likely to see a significant drop is sales or revenue from a downturn in a single country.

The same holds true for licensing agreements. While core business sales may drop at any given time for any number of reasons, it's possible for a decline in core sales to be cushioned by revenue generated via licensing agreements. These are the types of supplemental revenue streams which corporations to strive for in order to enhance their revenue stability (this is usually a common practice amongst well-run organizations).

The added benefit of diversifying revenue streams is a potential for higher growth rates. While a company with a single source of revenue is limited in the ways it can achieve fast growth rates, a company with multiple revenue sources can grow its business much faster simply because it has multiple growth opportunities. This type of favorable situation should not be overlooked, as it is in the best interest of shareholders for companies to create these types of opportunities.

Maximize Free Cash Flow. Free cash flow is basically the money that a business is able to retain after all liabilities and costs associated with continuing operations have been met. Any company with free cash flow that is consistently negative is unlikely to last over the long haul. This is because free cash flow is the blood of a business that allows it to continue financing its operations.

Without it, companies are almost certain to go bankrupt eventually (it's possible for bankruptcy to be delayed indefinitely through new common stock issuances, the raising of debt, or the selling of strategic assets).

Generally, there are three basic ways that a business can increase its free cash flow.

    1. It could increase its total sales volume.

2. It could raise product prices to improve its profit margins.
3. It could make an attempt to improve the efficiency of its operations.

Of these three possibilities, the first and last possibilities are generally considered to be the best options. This is because both taking measures to increase sales volume and improving operational efficiencies can have a very great impact on a company's bottom line and free cash flow.

> *"Free cash flow is the blood of a business that allows it to continue financing its operations."*

While the benefits of increasing sales are self-explanatory, the long-term benefits of operational efficiencies are sometimes not so. By definition, being operationally efficient involves the process of minimizing waste in a business while maximizing resource capabilities, in order to deliver high quality products to customers at the lowest possible cost.

These efficiencies are measured through specific fundamental metrics, as categorized by the company's core business and industry. Some traditional metrics include inventory turnover, overhead efficiency, cycle time, and cost of goods sold.

Improving operational efficiencies is actually a key element of supply chain management. The idea is that improving the efficiency of operations, a company will be able to become more profitable, and thus generate more money that it can reinvest elsewhere in the business.

If done correctly, improving operational efficiencies can also help a company to better position itself for a possible market or economic downturn. This is possible because efficient companies have a much better chance of surviving through difficult economic environments than their less efficient competitors due to larger profit margins, greater productivity, and potentially lower labor costs.

Align Management & Shareholder Goals. This is possible through compensating top company executives and officers with a combination of both cash and equity compensation.

By issuing stock compensation that matures after a specific number of years, the company can ensure that top management will act in the best interest of shareholders for as long as it takes for the stock options or stock holdings to mature at a minimum. This is a great way to align the interests of executive management with the interests of the overall company and its respective shareholders.

Stock-based compensation also serves as a great incentive to encourage executives to work harder as their actions could help to increase their own wealth as the share price of the company stock appreciates.

As an added bonus, equity compensation is great for the corporation from a cash perspective as payment via equity compensation is a non-cash payment. By compensating top management in the form of stock options and equity packages, these organizations would effectively be able to conserve their cash levels (at the cost of a higher future count of shares outstanding).

Communicate With Shareholders. When it comes to company shareholders, it is always better to keep an open channel and communicate regularly. There should not be any major surprises for shareholders, especially when it comes to negative surprises (if share prices of a company drop heavily on sudden bad news that should have been predictable, it often leads to class-action lawsuits). Also, when trying to increase the perceived value of a company, it really helps to have honest management that tells the company story/situation in simple English.

A well-told story is much more likely to be remembered and rewarded than a complicated story that's hard to understand. If shareholders understand the long term company plans and strategic objectives, they will be much less likely to react overly negatively should the company ever experience a short-term setback. It would also help to achieve a larger base of loyal shareholders which is good for the stability in the price of common shares.

Engaging with shareholders could also have some additional benefits. Given the influence wielded by large institutional shareholders, developing a good relationship could help to avert future problems which could arise such as pending approval for mergers and acquisitions, director elections, or even strategic use of resources. All of these things could be facilitated simply by regularly communicating and engaging with shareholders.

From the sections above, it should be clear that there are quite a few different measures which corporations can take to create additional value for shareholders. You should understand the advantages and disadvantages of all of these different measures so that you can spot companies with management that are skilled at using their resources effectively. It can be prove to be a great additional layer to your investment analysis/selection process.

When searching for a company that could be a great potential investment prospect, it is important to think about the steps the company has taken in order to create value. This means taking an in-depth look at a company's business model. We need to see and understand the impact of the different opportunities and risks taken by management. Only then could we make an educated decision about whether the company merits actual investment.

Familiarity with the company could really help speed up the time needed to make an investment decision. It's not by random chance that household companies and consumer durable companies tend to prove better investments than investments in many other industries.

There's just a lot more demand for shares in companies that are widely familiar, and this extra demand may be part of the reason that household names perform better on average. If you're interested to learn more about why it's beneficial to invest into companies and/or industries that you are familiar with, please read onto the next chapter.

Chapter 9:

Buy What You Understand

"If you can't explain it simply,
you don't understand it well enough."

– Albert Einstein

For some strange reason, many individual investors regularly talk themselves into believing that they must invest their money into obscure industries if they want to make extraordinary returns on their investments. Nothing could be further from the truth.

If you don't understand an industry well enough, then I would strongly recommend that you stay away from placing your money into that industry. This becomes especially true if you are unwilling to put in the time and effort necessary to thoroughly understand the inner workings of that industry.

If you aren't willing to put in that extra effort, you can actually improve your investment performance simply by sticking to what you understand well. One of the problems with putting money into an industry that you don't understand well is that you're putting yourself at a competitive disadvantage. If you aren't familiar with an industry, there's sure to be someone out there that has access to information that you don't.

Maybe you are unable to make sense of the strength of a specific company's business model in comparison with its competitors, or maybe you're unaware of the different trends going on in the industry that could potentially change the industry drastically in the near future. These can all be considered disadvantages, or potential risks arising from a lack of information.

These risks can be avoided simply by taking the time to make sure that you are familiar with the industry or company that you choose to invest in. Would you consider this to be a surprise? I don't think so. If you are a biotechnology scientist, then thoroughly understanding a company in the biotechnology sector could very well be easy for you.

The same goes for someone working in the auto industry; an auto-parts franchisee owner is much more likely to understand the auto industry better than perhaps the enterprise resource planning software industry. Why then, shouldn't you focus first on finding investment prospects in the industry or industries that you know best?

It makes no sense why people feel that they need to put their money in an industry outside the one that they may have many years of experience with. There certainly isn't any unwritten rule that says to do so. I guess the common notion that "the grass is always greener on the other side" applies here.

It seems that many people think that they can get better returns on their investments by analyzing other industries, or perhaps they just find other industries more exciting than their own. Truth is, we will never really know, nor does it really matter. The only thing that should matter to you is that this common fallacy helps us, as contrarians, to make more money!

So how do you know if you know an industry or company well enough to consider an investment? Don't sweat it, I'll show systematic process that you can follow to see if you're prepared! In fact, I'll even go so far as to throw in some basic analysis questions.

Keep an eye out for some of the key concepts from the previous chapters! Keep on reading below and you'll find that the process is actually very simple (so simple that even a caveman can do it).

THE PROCESS

Question One: Can you explain why you're considering investment in a certain industry or company in a simple and easy to understand sentence?

If yes: Good, it seems you understand why you're interested. Now it's necessary to do more research.

Start reading about the industry for a while and getting a feel for the major players, industry-related risks, and upcoming trends that may impact the industry as a whole.

If no: Keep on looking at other ideas until you can find one that you can easily describe and talk about. Do not settle for mediocre ideas or prospective investments that do not fall within your core competencies. Again, unless you are willing to put in the hours of detailed research and analysis to thoroughly understand a specific business, it's best to stick to what you know best.

Question Two: Are you willing do some research to understand important aspects or metrics that apply specifically to the industry or company you're interested in?

If yes: Good, any relevant information you can get your hands will help you to make a good decision. To come up with the best decision, it's always a good idea to talk to others that work in the industry you are considering. Many times, industry insiders may be able to let you know about competition in the space and emerging trends that have not yet become widely known. A good way to start your research process may be to set up *Google Alerts* on the topic or company of interest.

If no: Stop everything that you're doing and start over with the first step! You got to do some research! Don't be lazy: your financial future could very well be at risk if you continue to throw money at investment ideas without even doing an ounce of research.

Question Three: Is the company that you're interested in have good financials and management with a proven track record for successfully managing businesses?

If yes: Compare the financial metrics, business model, and management with those of its competitors. If you would like a reference for some of the different metrics to look at, consider referring back to chapter three. Also consider looking into learning more about any industry-specific metrics which may apply to your prospective company.

If no: This could still be a good investment, but it would be better to tread more carefully. Do some more research before even considering making a decision. Sometimes companies with poor financials can still make great investments, especially if they have emerged due to some special corporate-driven event such as a merger, spin-off, corporate restructuring, or partial spin-off. It also helps if there is an activist investor involved with the particular company.

Question Four: Is the company trading at a sizable discount of at least twenty-five percent below your fair value calculation or conservative future growth projections?

If yes: Great, this discount is called your margin of safety. Should your analysis be wrong or should the fundamentals of the underlying business change, by incorporating a margin of safety, you still allow yourself to have some room for error. Keep in mind that the larger the margin of safety the less likely will you incur a loss on the investment opportunity. At the same time, a 25% discount may not be enough of a discount for companies situated in cyclical industries. For this reason, the 25% discount rule is just a rule-of-thumb and it may be better to look for even larger discounts in certain cases.

If no: Consider looking for other alternatives if possible unless, perhaps, you have strong conviction that there may be a sharp price appreciation in the near future due to some special event or circumstance (i.e. pending spin-off, merger arbitrage scenario, potential special distribution, activist influence, anticipated new product launch, etc.) Discounts of 25% or more can prove to be very difficult to find for top-performing companies, so in certain cases it may be better to decide to buy a wonderful company at a reasonable price instead of an okay company at a wonderful price.

Question Five: Are you willing to hold onto your investment long enough for the price movement that you're expecting to actually occur?

If yes: Good--there's always the possibility that the price movement you're waiting for will take a while to occur or possibly even move against you. If you aren't willing to wait long enough for your idea to work out, there's a good chance your investment results will suffer. You always want to keep your investment horizon in mind every time you enter into a new position. At the same time, however, you want to regularly re-analyze the investment prospect to ensure that there is no material change within the company that may impact your original investment conclusion.

If no: What's wrong with you! Haven't you learned anything from any of the previous chapters? If you aren't willing to wait for a price movement, I suggest you go back to the first chapter and start reading this book again! I hope that my statement drives the point home: patience and discipline is the key to any successful investment strategy. Without it, you drastically reduce your chances of success in the investing game.

Question Six: Would you be willing to commit a sizable portion of your portfolio into this specific position or investment if needed?

If yes: Perfect! This is type of conviction you need to have before going into any investment. Chances are you would not be willing to put up a large amount of money into a position that you've done little research on. Getting into this mindset will help to force you to only focus on your best ideas or those with the highest probability of success. If this type of position moved against you, this level of conviction will also help you to have the courage to add to the falling position in order to average down the cost-basis.

If no: You seem to have the attention span of a gold-fish, but that's okay. I'll make it so easy to remember that you'll never forget it again. The best way to structure a portfolio is by allocating the majority of your available capital to only your best five to ten ideas! That's it, no tricks, and no surprises. Using concentrated portfolios is one of the best ways to ensure that you conduct the in-depth research that you need to find potential winning investment opportunities. It also, on average, allows you to generate above-average investment returns over the long-term.

This is as simple as it gets! Since you only want to allocate money to your best ideas, it should make sense that you should always be willing to allocate a good chunk of your portfolio into a single position (even though you ultimately might end up not doing so, you should still always be prepared).

Question Seven: Are the earnings of the business you're considering stable and consistent?

If yes: Now we're getting somewhere! Predictability of earnings is great, but it gets even better when the share price of a predictable company falls due to some short-term set-back or market sell-off. These are the perfect times for opportunistic contrarians to pick up shares on the cheap. The key here is to ensure that any problem being faced by the predictable company is fixable and not a symptom of an underlying critical fundamental flaw.

If no: Although your prospective idea could very well prove to be profitable, it's better to tread carefully. Make sure to consider any alternative ideas first before choosing to pursue an investment in this particular opportunity. Consistency in earnings over an extended period of time is the clearest sign of a strong business with a potential competitive edge. If you still want to proceed to invest in a company with unpredictable earnings, try to get an estimate of normalized earnings. Normalized earnings are typically calculated by taking the average of the typical earnings during a standard business cycle (usually a period of 5-7 years) and adding in growth elements as applicable.

Question Eight: Do you know when and under what circumstance you will sell your investment?

If yes: Awesome! Having an exit strategy is a necessity. You should always go into an investment with set exit criteria. You're criteria can be as simple as the notion that you'll sell if your investment appreciates fifteen percent or more above your fair value calculation. The point is, you should have some type of strategy that you could easily replicate consistently. It's also important to regularly re-assess your original investment thesis as material changes occur.

If no: You may want to refer back to chapter six. There's an entire section there which talks about different strategies that can be used to help limit losses. I strongly suggest you look to learn more about how to mitigate risk and adopt a more disciplined investment screening process.

Well, there you have it. No tricks and certainly nothing too complex. I'm not even asking for a donation (a cookie would be nice though!). I've just shown you the same simple process that I use myself when analyzing a prospective investment. This is the SAME process that has allowed me to consistently achieve above-average returns, and now you can too! You can see an even more detailed version of this process by checking out *The Warren Buffet Way.*

So, what next? Well, let's talk about some of the added benefits that buying what you know can bring to your research process:

You can check demand yourself. If you're looking at an investment into a retail company that you know and understand very well, you could potentially visit some of the store's physical locations to check customer traffic. To better understand what I mean by this, let's consider the example of Express, Inc., a specialty American apparel retailer that was founded in 1980 and is currently headquartered in Columbus, Ohio.

Express, Inc. is a pretty common sight throughout many shopping malls across the country. If you wanted to check the demand for Express products, it would be pretty easy to get a good idea simply by checking the customer traffic at some its outlet mall locations. While there, you could also take the time to check the customer traffic at competing clothing retailers to spot which retailers seem to be garnering the most consumer interest. (I love using the example of Express because it's one of my favorite clothing retailers, both due to my good experience with it in my investment portfolio as of this writing, as well as their stylish clothing which I really enjoy wearing).

In fact, I would actually advise for you to visit the mall on a regular basis, such as perhaps once a month at the minimum. As Peter Lynch once advocated in *One Up On Wall Street*, the mall is a great place to come up with a list of prospective investments within the consumer products industry. By visiting the mall regularly, you will start to notice consumer buying trends, customer spending habits, and possibly even changing trends in fashion.

You can check the quality of the merchandise. Have you ever been in a situation where you knew a certain product was going to be a success months before it actually became a hit? I know I have, and I've wanted to hit myself over the head for not putting some of my money into these types of ideas that I had a strong feeling would succeed.

It's a common reaction. When we miss an opportunity that could have made us a considerable amount of money, we always tend to blame ourselves—even when that blame may not always have been justified.

Well, here's the reality: I don't want to make the same type of mistake again, and neither should you. One measure that we can take to limit the number of great opportunities that pass us by is by keeping a close eye on the types of products that are being sold quickly at popular shopping outlets. Keeping track of the latest best-selling products may very well prove to be a goldmine for ideas on great prospective investments.

One of the best benefits of buying products of a household company is the ability to actually assess the quality of company products. You rarely, if ever, would get to do this with companies that you have little knowledge of or access to. When it comes to researching apparel companies like Express, this ability to physically assess products becomes a huge potential advantage (especially when combined with detailed financial analysis and discussion with management).

Over time, the quality of merchandise available at stores could become either better or worse. By taking the time to visit physical stores, you can be one of the first people to see this potential change, well before the changes in merchandise quality may have an impact on company sales or profitability.

If you're still in school, you have an even bigger advantage when it comes to buying what you know. This becomes especially true when it comes to investing in companies like clothing retailers. Teenagers and young adults that are still in school come across many different types of people almost every day, and this is exactly why this age group is best poised to stumble upon the winning investments.

The only reason we don't regularly hear about "star" teen-aged investors is that most teenagers and young adults don't have the patience to thoroughly learn about detailed financial analysis. They also do not normally possess the emotional discipline required to succeed in the investing game. However, if this were not the case, I wouldn't be surprised if a teenager or young adult with these characteristics were able to outperform other investment professionals.

> *"Teenagers and young adults that are still in school come across many different types of people almost every day, and this is exactly why this age group is best poised to stumble upon the winning investments."*

Since teenagers and young adults tend to regularly visit the mall, they tend to have a better understanding of the types of clothes or accessories other people are wearing and which brands people seem to like and dislike. Sometimes, companies that sell popular brands may be performing exceedingly well, but the market may not have yet caught on and bid up the share prices of the company accordingly.

These are the types of disparities which we, as contrarians should always try to look for. If you are able to do this right, you could very well find yourself with some great winners. So what are you waiting for? Get out there and go make me proud! Find your own winning investment. You may very well be surprised with how fun it may prove to be.

It's relatively easy to spot promotional activities. When you visit stores frequently, you often start to get a sense of which company is selling its products well, and which companies are struggling. Any time you see a company initiating a huge promotional campaign; it can only mean one of two things.

First, it could mean that the company is trying to attract new customers to come in and check out the store. Second, it could mean that the company isn't currently selling its products too well, and so has initiated a new pricing scheme or promotional campaign in order to get rid of unwanted inventory.

By regularly visiting the physical locations of different companies, you start to be able to distinguish between promotional campaigns that will eventually prove to be successful, and those designed simply to stop the bleeding.

This is the type of information that "professional investors" or "sophisticated investors" are unlikely to take the time to learn about, and it is this informational edge that could put you at a potential advantage over the professionals.

It's possible to spot potential trends early on. Believe it or not, it's possible for ordinary people to spot trends in the marketplace well before the experts on Wall Street even get an idea that something is amiss. This is because few people in the world of high finance actually go out to visit physical company stores or locations (and even when they do, they are not always as adept at making sense of what they see as those of a younger age group may be).

Fundamental research on Wall Street is largely based on financial metrics and numbers. Wall Street experts only realize that a company is not doing as well as previously forecasted when they speak with company management or get a hold of the most recent sales/earnings numbers. These sources of information are simply not enough. Of course, experts may also conduct surveys and measure the results to get a rough idea of trends, but in most cases these surveys or polls do not have a large enough sample size to obtain a good reading of public opinion and overall sales results.

"It's possible for ordinary people to spot trends in the marketplace well before the experts on

> *Wall Street even get an idea that something is amiss."*

Retail investors, on the other hand, have an advantage over Wall Street experts in this aspect. Besides looking through corporate filings and reading through financial metrics and forecasts, retail investors have the unique opportunity to conduct an equivalent type of fundamental research just by eating out at a restaurant or comparing the quality of merchandise available at competing stores.

Fundamental research is all about the quality of a company's earnings and balance sheet, but if we can assess the strength or quality of the actual service or product that a company provides, this would definitely help us to understand the reason behind the company' s success or failure.

Since fundamental research aims to provide us with this same type of research, it would be reasonable to say that physically analyzing company products and services is equivalent to a traditional fundamental analysis. The only difference is in the way we obtained that information.

So now that the benefits of buying what you know should be clear, it's on to the closing remarks. Buying what you know is a great strategy for those investors that find the investment research process to be boring. Generally, people are much more interested in learning more about companies or industries that they are familiar with then they are for learning more about an industry that would not really impact their daily lives.

It's for this reason, that I strongly advocate for those unwilling to take the time to learn about new industries to simply stick to the handful of companies and industries that they know best. This simple trick alone could save these types of investors from tons of unnecessary headaches and potential investment losses.

Chapter 10:

The Contrarian Way

"I always knew I was going to be rich.
I don't think I doubted it for a second."

– Warren Buffet

The contrarian way is all about following what you believe in, even if it means going against the thinking of the crowd. When it comes to investments, this means that if the crowd is excessively pessimistic about something, then that something may very well merit additional research. The same can be said for cases where the crowd is overly optimistic.

Being a contrarian means having the strength to stand alone when you have to, even when it proves to be exceedingly difficult to do so. There always seems to be safety in numbers, but you would be surprised at how many times the crowd is wrong while those standing alone in their judgment ultimately end up being the ones that are right. Galileo, Einstein, Gandhi, Columbus, Oprah, Thomas Edison, Martin Luther King Jr., Steve Jobs, Walt Disney, the list of these types of examples is endless.

It is only those people in this world that have the strength to question the status quo and public perception that have the power to change things. You too can one day become this type of person if you truly put your mind to it.

> *"It is only those people in this world that have the strength to question the status quo and public perception that have the power to change things."*

Every few decades, there comes a person, a product, or a new philosophy that once introduced, changes everything. Contrarians are the types of people that often strive for these types of reality-shattering changes. It's true that those strong enough to believe that they make a difference in the world are the ones that actually change it. History has shown this to be true, time and time again.

To bring my point home, I'd like to share with you three incredible stories. The first story is about changing your daily habits. There are so many people out there in the world that will live out their lives, never truly understanding the significant impact that small changes in your daily routines can have upon your life. I don't want you, the reader of this book, to be one of those people.

This first story begins with me as a teenager, living in a small town on the outskirts of a big city in New Jersey. Growing up, I was never really interested in reading books or paying attention to the news, let alone considering potential investments. In those days, I always believed that watching the news was a complete waste of time.

It was always the same story over and over again: some political tension brewing in Congress, a string of deaths occurring somewhere in the country, or the occasional robbery involving masked criminals. Books were no different, with the same basic themes being recycled over and over again. "How could any of these things possibly impact my daily life", I remember thinking. I spent a large majority of my childhood and teenage years shackled down by this narrow-minded thinking.

It was only when I entered college that my thinking started to change. I began to get involved much more with my community and neighborhood, and this is when things suddenly began to become much clearer. I started to become much more interested in what was happening around the world around me. I wanted to understand why things were the way they were, and what I could personally do to potentially make a difference.

I started to understand how everything was inter-connected and how a natural disaster in some seemingly remote area on the other side of the globe could have a potential world-wide impact. I went from being somewhat ignorant of the world to slowly gathering a much deeper and conclusive understanding.

All of this was possible because I set aside some time everyday to spend time thinking about future possibilities and reading to increase my awareness. One small change in my daily routine is what made all the difference!

Nowadays, I start off every day spending at least an hour on furthering my own education and understanding of the world. This involves reading books on persuasion techniques, presentation skills, investments, negotiations, historical events and people, as well as keeping up to date on the latest news in various industries, technology and retail being two of my favorite.

All of these things not only give me plenty of things to talk about, but it also has helped me to develop my soft skills dramatically. I've found myself as a successful investor, an author, and a skilled presenter. The changes that I've undergone have drastically changed my life for the better, and the best part is that you could do the same!

All it takes is spending some time to develop new good habits. Your habits could be as simple reading something new everyday to as complex as prioritizing your family and work obligations. You need to realize that it is not always just about work-life balance. The key isn't to separate your work life from your personal life, but to get involved with work-life integration.

You need to find a way to seamlessly merge your work life and personal lives together in a way that is beneficial rather than detrimental. Some examples could be bringing your family along on a work trip to an exotic location or finding creative solutions that allow you to be able to work from home more often. The key is to stop finding excuses for why your two lives need to be separate and finding ways that they can co-exist simultaneously instead. If you are able to do this, you'll likely find yourself much happier and relaxed than you have ever been.

Before anything, it is very important to find out what is important in your life. It is only by identifying the essentials or things in your life that you love that you can figure out exactly how to eliminate the non-essentials, and it is this process of elimination which will ultimately change your life. By eliminating the unnecessary things you'll be left only to focus on what's important, and that is what makes all the difference. In the same way that my life has changed by adopting new good habits and changing my perspective, I'm sure that your life can change for the better as well.

The second story focuses around always being happy for what you have instead of focusing on what you don't. Unless you are the richest person in the world, there will always be someone out there that has more money or resources than you. So why should you let this difference bring you down instead of motivating you to do better instead?

Doesn't it make more sense to just make the most of what you do have, and maybe educate yourself on the different steps that you can take to expand your means while doing what you love? Knowledge and experience are what enable people to achieve success, so these should always be the focus of any endeavor you wish to pursue.

This second story is about a now well-known woman who had experienced tremendous financial struggles early in her life. Abandoned at birth by her mother, sexually and physically abused by her foster parents, and addicted to drugs, this young woman was a complete mess.

She found herself in and out of rehabilitation for cocaine abuse. She was forced to steal, to deceive, and to cheat, all just to get enough money to feed herself a few meals a day. And the worst part? She was raped at the young age of thirteen, eventually giving birth to a still-born baby at fourteen. Her life was filled with struggles and misery, the type of which most of us would never even begin to truly understand.

Now, if this same woman was still living a life filled with struggles and financial difficulties today, few would blame her. They would most likely blame her childhood or the environment she was exposed to at such a young age.

But what if I told you that this same woman is now one of the most influential, respected, and successful women in the world today? Any ideas on who this once misfortunate woman is today? You guessed it; she's the multi-billionaire and media mogul Oprah Winfrey!

This is the power of positive thinking. Focus on how you can make the most of your experiences and current resources, and you will find yourself much better off in the long run. Instead of despising herself and what she had become as a result of her childhood, Oprah focused on the positives. She took her tragic experiences and used them to inspire others!

She found her passion in motivating others that were currently experiencing tragic circumstances similar to her own childhood. This passion is what led to the creation of Oprah's talk-show, ultimately leading to her rise to fame, glory, and success.

Despite her success, Oprah still stays close to her roots, giving back to those less fortunate than her, enabling others to gain access to the same types of opportunities that she herself had not had access to as a child.

I am amazed that out of so much struggle and difficulty, it is possible to still emerge a better person than before. A transformation like this certainly does not happen overnight. It's always a slow transition, but one which can have the biggest impact on your confidence, thinking, and aspirations.

You too should try to follow in the footsteps of this truly fantastic woman. Focus on what you have instead of what you don't have. Only then will you be able to find your passion and develop the confidence and positive thinking needed to eventually find success. Who knows, maybe you too can one day become the topic of a truly motivating and inspirational story. I sure hope you do!

The third and final story is about doing what you can to motivate and inspire others around you. Often times, people don't remember what you say, but remember how you make them feel. This is why people are moved much more by touching stories than they are by logic or facts.

This last story is about a now-deceased tech entrepreneur by the name of Steve Jobs (1955-2011). During his lifetime, Steve Jobs was the perfect embodiment of marketing genius and true passion. If you've never heard of this renowned entrepreneur before, I strongly suggest you come out of the cave you've been hiding in over the last decade-and-a-half.

For those of you who don't know (the cave dwellers), Steve Jobs was the founder of Apple Inc., a Cupertino, California-based company that designs, manufacturers, and distributes media and personal computing products, alongside various other electronic gadgets and software. Some of the company's most well-known products include the Macintosh, iPod, iPhone, iTunes, iPad, and iMac.

Steve Jobs was a true visionary. During his lifetime, he helped found three companies: Apple, NeXT (now part of Apple), and Pixar, two of which ultimately turned into huge success stories (I'll let you take a guess as to which two). Years after his death, the technology industry is still feeling the loss of his presence.

People that knew Steve Jobs personally will tell you varying stories about both his charismatic and truly terrifying personality. Jobs was a hard-core perfectionist, always demanding the highest quality work from all of those around them.

Many described his charisma as truly electrifying. He had the ability to put your hair on end with his performances which often conveyed a flair for the dramatic. He could bend reality and manipulate people at will in order to get what he wanted.

This "reality-distortion field" as Job's ability was described as, was created by a combination of charm, passion, exaggeration, marketing genius, and persistence. It allowed Jobs to easily motivate, inspire, and manipulate people as necessary. He could sway over the public, generate excitement for new product launches, and strike the opposition right where it hurt—all in a day's work.

His presentations were simple, yet filled with visuals, rhetoric, videos, stories, and spectacular performances. People don't enjoy listening to long lectures, looking at numerical charts, or making sense of complex data. They enjoy simplicity, stories, and descriptive language, and this is just what Steve Jobs provided for his audience. He was a master salesman, taking his audience through an emotional roller coaster, filled with suspense, surprise, awe, and excitement.

Despite his famous talent and world-wide recognition, there were plenty of people that were truly terrified by Steve's presence. When he didn't need something from you, Jobs was blunt with his criticisms, never hesitating to tell you what he really thought about a product or idea, even if it meant dropping the occasional F-bomb or hurting your feelings.

This dual personality was both a blessing and a curse for the famous entrepreneur. While it created an environment that demanded work of the highest quality, it also posed many conflicts in the workplace. Employees were often pitted in competition with each other, strong criticisms were regularly thrown about, and time was wasted amongst the confusion.

Despite this, Steve was still always able to attract great employees, partly because he strongly because his passion for his work was contagious. Jobs wanted to create beautiful products with elegant designs (inspired by his travels and understanding of Zen Buddhism), and he highly respected and praised anyone that had the talent to actually develop these types of products.

People are inspired by passion, and Jobs was the embodiment of passion. His desire for designing beautiful products was unparalleled. If you wish to one day inspire others, you too must do what it takes to find your passion.

If you are able to present yourself as truly passionate about a topic or idea, your persuasive ability will increase dramatically. People will want to do whatever they can to make your aspirations a reality, even if they may have to make some sacrifices or adjustments of their own in order to help. Such was the case with Steve Jobs, and such would be the case for just about any passionate individual.

It's human nature. People love sensations that excite them, and passion serves to evoke these very emotions. Steve Jobs was a master at this. His passion for his work thrilled participants and by-standers alike.

When it comes to finding your passion, never settle. If you can't find what you're passionate about then you should just keep on searching. You'll know it when you find it. It's only once you find your life's calling that you will find yourself achieving the success you've always dreamed about. While people may not always remember what you say, they will always remember how you make them feel. This is the reality of the world we live in.

These three stories demonstrate the steps necessary to become a true contrarian. Being a contrarian is not easy, but it's definitely the only way to gain true recognition in a world filled with conformists.

This is what the contrarian way is all about. It's all about not being afraid to think differently, taking the time to educate yourself, focusing on what you believe in, and inspiring others around you in the process. It is only when you've mastered all of these things that you can truly call yourself a *Master of the Contrarian Way*. So what are you waiting for? Get out there and **change the world**. You'll be glad you did.

I hope this book has helped to inspire you to succeed both in investing and in life. Feel free to share your stories and progress by sending a message to the author on Twitter!

AFTERWORD:

How to Manage Your Money

"Money, like emotions, is something you must
control to keep your life on the right track."

– Natasha Munson

What is money exactly? Many people
think they know what it is, but when asked to
describe it, they draw a blank. What about you? Can
you come up with the right words to describe it?
Well, if you can't, don't worry because today I
would like to take the time to further your
understanding of money. I'd also like to take the
time to explain to you some of the many different
ways that it can be managed to help you to
accumulate even more of it.

Money is used as a form of payment to purchase
goods and services. It is essentially a common
currency, something which most people value
equally. It is because most people place the same
value on money that can be used to facilitate
exchange and trade.

This brings up a very important question. Where
does money get its value from? If you really think
about it, a one-hundred dollar bill is just a piece of
paper with some special ink on it, costing no more

than a few cents to actually produce. Knowing this, how does a hundred dollar bill get its value, as well....a hundred dollars?

Paper currencies like a dollar bill have no intrinsic value. They aren't worth anything as stand-alone items, and you can't use a dollar bill for any practical purposes. Metals like gold and silver, on the other hand, actually possess intrinsic value. They can be used to actually make things. Gold and silver can be sculpted or shaped into trophies, rings, watches, earrings, and many other decorative items. The same is not the case for a dollar bill.

Paper currencies only possess value because they are backed by the credit and faith of the United States Government. Should the U.S. Government magically disappear tomorrow, then the remaining paper currency would become utterly worthless. This is the extent of the value of a dollar bill. It's only worth something as long as the public has faith in the stability and competence of the national government.

So now that we understand what money is, let's talk about some of the different steps we can take to make more of it. The formula for making money is actually very simple: live below your means and find ways to expand your means.

The living below your means aspect should be self-explanatory. It simply means spending less than you earn, and doing all you can to live a debt-free lifestyle (there are some good types of debt that we'll talk about later). The purpose of living below your means is to actually keep a portion of the money that you make.

What good does making a lot of money do for you if at the end of the day, you aren't really able to retain any of it? In that type of situation, should your income be affected for any reason, you would quickly end up broke. This is the reason why living below your means is such a useful strategy in order to accumulate wealth over the long-term. *The Millionaire Next Door* explains the epitome of this concept with great real-life examples. The expanding your means part, however, is a bit more difficult to truly comprehend.

Expanding your means describes the process of finding new ways to make money and increase your income. This could involve investments into companies, real estate, businesses, or possibly even the development of new income streams. The point is to create an income source that supplements any income that you either current generate, or expect to generate in the near future.

When it comes to making money, the trick to making more is to avoid trading in your time and energy for a paycheck, as well as find ways to better control and reduce your tax liabilities. Any time you are trading your time for a paycheck, there are always limitations to just how much money you can make. This limitation is your time.

The amount of time you can work is finite, and easily quantifiable. Since there are only twenty-four hours in the day, that is the maximum amount of hours that you can work on any given day (assuming you are able to function without sleep).

It's physically impossible to work any more hours than there are in the day, and this is where the problem lies. So many people nowadays, focus on their careers and on keeping their jobs that they forget this limitation. They fantasize about becoming rich, yet don't even take the first step in the right direction. They focus on working more hours and possible working over-time for the increased hourly pay rate.

Yes, doing these things allow you to make more money, but would still be trading in your time and effort for a paycheck. With salaried or hourly position, there's a cap on just how much money you can actually make, and this is the problem. This idea is explained in much more detail in *Rich Dad, Poor Dad*.

The only time it makes sense to work harder and longer is if you are either working for yourself or are being paid based on the amount of money you generate for the business that you work for (some type of commission-based structure). Only then could you actually find yourself making substantially more money by trading in your time for money.

In addition to its time limitations, working for a salary also reduces your control over the amount of taxes you pay. This is because salaries are automatically withheld by the company you work for in accordance to your income level and dependent status. That's the purpose of the W9 and similar forms that you're asked to fill out when you first start at a new job. These forms are used to inform the company just how much of your paycheck should be withheld for tax purposes.

This is the problem with trading in your labor for a paycheck. There are some significant limitations both from a time-based and tax-based standpoint. If you, the reader, which to overcome these obstacles, the solution would be to have your money work for you instead of you yourself working for money.

While the earned income taxation rate is generally constant, unearned income generally is not so. Businesses and investments allow individuals with many more opportunities for tax deductions, loss provisions, and potential reimbursements. For a quick example, any expenses that may occur as necessary part of operating a business (i.e. travel, gas, food, and supply expenses) can be tax deductible, thus reducing overall tax liabilities.

These same tax deduction opportunities are not available for those that trade in their time/effort for a paycheck or job. And the best part? If you set up your business correctly and have trustworthy people working for you, you may get paid to do almost no work at all! That's right, let me say it again, **no work at all**.

Of course, this does not mean that you should not check over how your business is functioning every once in a while. I'm just stating that the bulk of the operations would be managed by your employees, allowing you to take time off and focus on the other passions of your life.

Instead of attempting to generate income from only a day job, it makes much more sense to establish multiple income sources, thus reducing the importance of a day job as the primary method to meet your financial obligations. One method to do this is to create multiple income streams is to find opportunities which allow for the establishment of residual income.

There are quite a few ways to do this. One way is through starting up a business in an industry known for having repeat customers. Another is to find an investment opportunity that allows for a sustainable long-term return. This could come in the form of long-term corporate or government bonds, investment funds, or even investments into private companies.

Although investing is a great way to expand your means, it does come with its own set of risks. When it comes to trying to expand your means by investing, doing your homework is a very important first step. Knowledge is one of the most important factors that could make the difference between actually making money versus losing nearly all of it on a slap-shod investment choice. This is why I would generally recommend individuals to not use debt when considering investments, especially if they do not possess in-depth knowledge of their investment prospects.

If you really think about it, debt is a very unusual thing. Although debt is generally viewed negatively (for good reason), there are some types of debt that are actually good instead of bad. The typical bad types of debt include debt that is incurred for purposes other than to increase overall income.

These types of debt include credit card debt, student loans, car loans, and under certain circumstances, even mortgage loans (such as for primary residencies). All of these types of debt put a strain upon an individual's cash flow due to fact that the principal must be paid back with accumulated interest. Because of its impact on a person's ability to retain income, these are the types of debt which should be avoided whenever possible.

In the same way that there are bad types of debt, there are also some good types of debt. These good types of debt involve debt incurred for the purpose of expanding your means. Some examples include loans taken out to purchase rental real estate property or to start up a sustainable business. Although these types of debt do involve a degree of risk, they are much better than consumer and student debt because this debt can be used to quickly increase your income.

An added benefit is that debt for income purposes can often help to amplify your return. For example, a loan taken out in order to purchase a rental real estate property allows you to be able to participate in the rental income generated from renting out the property to tenants, without putting down the capital to purchase out the property outright (all you would need is the down payment, and the loan would cover the rest).

The reason why loans that are taken out for investment purposes are better than consumer loans is due to the rationale behind these loans. Consumer loans are available to allow individuals to live beyond their means (spending more money than they can currently afford), while investment loans are used to increase future income or maintain an existing revenue stream. One type of loan ultimately helps to make people poorer by reducing their net worth, while the other aims to make people wealthier by increasing their total income. The two are like complete opposites: yin and yang, true and false, yes and no.

That's it. That is the difference between the thinking between the wealthy and the poor. Poor people take on debt to increase the amount of stuff that they can buy, while the rich focus on taking on debt to increase the amount of income they ultimately bring home. One side focuses on living beyond their means while the other side focuses on living beneath it. Which side will you choose?

If you want to become very wealthy one day, it definitely makes the most sense to follow in the footsteps of the rich. That means finding new sources of income, preferably the type that allows you to make money without trading in your own time and labor. Only then will you live to see the type of wealth that you've always wished you had.

I hope this section has helped to further your understanding of money, and helped you to realize the distinctions between the thoughts of the rich and the not-so-rich. If it has, then this section has served its purpose. I wish all of the readers the best with their future endeavors and look forward to hearing stories about how this book has changed their lives for the better…

About the Author

KETUL KOTHARI is an accomplished investor with more than a decade of experience with the financial markets. He is an avid disciple of value / contrarian investing and has spent many years closely analyzing hedge fund and insider activity.

If you wish to connect with the author, you may contact him on Twitter @kkothari2

CPSIA information can be obtained at www.ICGtesting.com
Printed in the USA
LVOW01s1819050615

441366LV00031B/1017/P